... ar
how to communicate!

---Do your relationships get stuck or fade away?

---Do you have difficulty resolving disagreements with others?

---Are you afraid to speak your mind for fear of what might happen?

---Do you get into trouble because you say things you don't really mean?

---Do problems or people upset you more than they should?

---Do you wish you had ways and means of developing higher quality relationships?

If you find yourself leaning toward a "yes" answer to these questions, if you try to reach others who lean toward a "yes," then you will probably find this book rewarding.

Acknowledgements

To Ingrid, Chris and Becca Dilley; Carol Miller; Peg Olson; Jayne Vande Hey; and Jim Lee; for encouragement, support and valuable assistance in bringing this project to a successful completion:

To Ruth Lytton and Eileen Arndt for assistance in typing the manuscript, and to Jonnie Sue Hyde and Bonnie Gunnon for editorial expertise:

To the many others—friends, family members, students and colleagues—who must here go unnamed, yet who in no small way contributed to the final result:

To those whose lives provided the substance that gives life and meaning to the text, and to the many authors and workshop leaders whose works inspired me and gave me direction (some are mentioned in the Postscript):

To my mother for continued support these many years:

To all of you, I say, "Thank You!" Without your help this book could not have been written. I shall always be grateful.

...and I thought I knew how to communicate!

Exploring Fresh Choices in Relating

by

Josiah Dilley

Copyright ©1985
EDUCATIONAL MEDIA CORPORATION®
P.O. Box 21311
Minneapolis, MN 55421

(under special arrangements with the author)

Library of Congress Catalog Card No. 85-070456

ISBN 0-932796-17-6

Printing (Last Digit)

10 9 8 7 6 5 4 3 2 1

No part of this book may be reproduced or used in any form
without the expressed permission of the publisher in writing.
Manufactured in the United States of America.

Production editor

Don L. Sorenson

Graphic design

Earl Sorenson

Cover Illustration

Mary McKee

Table of Contents

... and I thought I knew how to communicate!

Introduction

Many of us get ahead in the world (some more than others), but few of us escape hostility, cold-war relationships, conflict or frustration along the way. We win a few (leaving hard feelings behind) and lose a few (getting hurt in the process). We go through stormy sessions from which no one comes out ahead (wondering how life could get this crazy). Loneliness, despair, abuse and divorce all testify to the difficulties we encounter.

At first glance, it doesn't make sense that so many people suffer emotional pain. More forms of help—books, magazine articles, courses, experts—are available now than ever before. What prevents people from making effective use of this help? For one thing, habit!

Psychology has demonstrated that behavior that was well-learned at an early age has greater strength than behavior of more recent origin. For example, we may now learn to express anger in non-abusive ways, yet revert to destructive patterns when our anger is aroused. We may now realize that we need to speak up when taken advantage of, yet lapse into silence as we have habitually done in the past. What happens is that old habits intrude, preventing us from making fresh choices that could lead us in new directions, and we may not even be aware that habit has taken over.

It would be absurd to claim that people can't get along with each other. They can and do, up to a point, and then in some way get stuck. They may become embarrassed about communicating affection, or defensive when dealing with differences of opinion, or withdrawn when their feelings get hurt or arrogant with their know-it-all manner or. . . . They lack the skills to move beyond their habits or to communicate in more effective ways.

One reason they get stuck is that important communication skills are not taught in school or home. For example, little attention is paid to developing children's abilities to listen without judging or to accept criticism constructively. The authoritarian models provided by teachers and parents do not teach democratic ways of settling differences and resolving conflicts among equals.

Another reason is that much of what people see and hear in the media tends to be ineffective as a means of developing healthy interpersonal relationships. Take television, for example. When Archie Bunker from *All in the Family* calls his son-in-law a "meathead," the audience laughs. The same is true when the noted host of a late-night talk show refers to his side kick as "two martini breath" or "son of a camel." The kinds of dialogue that amuse—put downs, sarcasm, insinuations, play on words, sexual double talk, cover ups—are certainly not the stuff out of which quality relationships are built. Neither are cop-and-robber dialogues, interviews with sports figures, running commentaries by announcers at sporting events or the hysterical outbursts between characters in soap operas.

. . . and I thought I knew how to communicate! deals with habit, awareness and choice. From my years of experience as a teacher, counselor, parent and consultant, I have assembled a collection of materials—verbal, pictorial, experiential—that people can use to improve their ability to relate with others. These materials contain 1) examples and descriptions of specific thought, feeling, and communication habits that are often self-defeating, 2) exercises for self-awareness, 3) descriptions of alternative ways of speaking and listening, 4) activities for practice, and 5) ideas for strengthening one's ability to move through life in satisfying ways. My thanks to the many people who have been involved in the creating and field testing of these materials.

The ideas and techniques presented here have a solid foundation in the literature associated with Gestalt, Psychosynthesis, Communications Theory and General Semantics. (A list of references appears in the Postscript.) I hope that . . . *and I thought I knew how to communicate!* gives you as much satisfaction in reading and doing as it has to me in writing. May your journey through these pages be rewarding!

CHAPTER 1

Habit:
A Cause of Conflict

Interpersonal conflicts develop over money, friends, possessions, places, work, religion, personal qualities, politics— almost anything that has meaning in life.

Tommy: You're dumb!

Jane: I'm not dumb. I'm just as smart as you are.

Tommy: You are too dumb. Just ask your sister.

Jane: I'm not dumb and you know it. Stop saying that.

Tommy: Dummy, dummy, dummy.

Jane: OK smarty! How much is 57 times 98?
etc., etc., etc.

One day my neighbor's son held his arm high above his head and said, "Big, like this." His older brother, who was much taller, replied, "That's not big, that's little. Don't you know anything?" His younger brother replied defensively, "Is too, big." "You don't know what big is," his older brother retorted, and left the yard on his bike. As he left, his younger brother kept repeating defiantly, "Big, big, big."

Arguments like these begin when a person makes a statement of fact that person believes to be true, only to have that statement rejected by another person. "I'm right and you're wrong" then becomes the theme for both. Evidence is often introduced to defend "true" right or to attack "false" right. It doesn't seem to matter that some of the evidence may be unrelated to the original statement. Let's listen to an argument between husband and wife.

He: You spent too much money on those shoes!

She: It was not too much. I got a good deal on those shoes and I needed them.

He: It was more than we could afford and you know it.

She: You waste money on yourself and then you have the nerve to tell me that I spend too much.

He: Quit trying to change the subject.

She: I'm not changing the subject. We're talking about what we can afford and we certainly can't afford that new stereo you bought.

He: We're not talking about the stereo. We're talking about you wasting money.

She: I didn't waste money. I already told you I got a good deal. I'm saying that you have no right to accuse me when you waste money on yourself.

He: You never deal with things we have to deal with. You always change the subject.

She: You're just like my father, always treating me like I'm not old enough to know a good deal when I see one.

With right/wrong arguments, there is no way to end the conflict without loss. One person is bound to lose self-respect, the argument itself, or some good feelings toward the other. To avoid these possibilities, one person often quits before the argument is finished. Both parties end up frustrated, and the unfinished conflict will likely reappear at a later date.

...and I thought I knew how to communicate!

Right/wrong conflicts can lead to hurt feelings, broken homes, emotional distress, rejection, verbal and physical abuse, and other expressions of anger ("I'll show her," "I'll never forgive you for this," or "I'll get you for that"). Sometimes the hurt doesn't show. People believe they have risen above such childish arguments and deny their feelings. In that case one would not hear the conflicting words. But below the surface, anger and resentment build.

Conflicts like these solve no problems, strain relationships, lead to noncooperation, severely reduce the quality of life, and are unnecessary. They occur out of some misguided notions about communication and some self-defeating reaction habits. When the misguided notions and reaction habits are changed, dialogue, not conflict, takes place; relationships are strengthened.

What are these misguided notions? One is that word statements of fact are necessarily tied to the facts themselves. People argue over the words in the mistaken belief that they are arguing over the facts. Consider the "big/not big" argument.

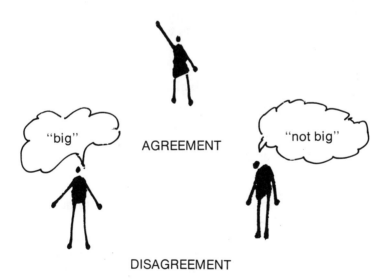

Both boys could see the younger one's arm raised above his head. Presumably there was agreement as to the location of his arm. Thus there was no argument over the facts. There was, however, an argument. That argument was over the rightness and wrongness of the words that were used in reference to those facts. One thought that "big" was a right word; the other thought "big" was wrong. The boys might maintain they were arguing over the facts. It seems clear to me that they were not.

The same idea holds true for the "money for shoes" argument. Both He and She agreed on the facts (She spent X dollars for Y pair of shoes at Z store). The conflict was over the words each used in reference to those facts.

The couple might protest and maintain that they were arguing, not over mere words, but over important issues. I could agree with them that there were important issues that they should discuss, and then point out that by getting into a right/wrong word argument they failed to focus on those issues in a way that could lead to a solution (and they put one more dent in their relationship).

Conflicts arise partly because people argue over words in the mistaken belief that they are arguing over facts, and partly because of their habits of reacting to certain word patterns.

How Conflict Habits Develop

As children we heard people naming things. A bottle of the white liquid that people drink is called "milk"; a black, furry animal that goes "Meow" is a "kitty." As we learned names, we learned facts (truths) about the world: "This animal is a kitty." "That blanket is blue." "The round seat with a hole is a potty." As time passed, we learned more names, and we learned other words as well. Soon we became skillful enough to put words together, following the patterns of those around us. Thus we, too, could state facts: "Baby sleep." "Stove hot." Sometimes when we used words that others didn't want us to use, we were corrected: "That's not bread, it's toast." "That's a truck, not a bus," and so forth.

In learning language, we learned that words are associated with things. We learned that when certain words are associated with particular things, they are true facts and therefore right. Other words are considered to be false and therefore wrong. We learned that people who speak untruths (wrong words) are corrected by others. We learned that people who use right words are accepted and sometimes rewarded.

In school these learnings were reinforced by teachers who gave out gold stars and smiles to children when they used the right words and who made red-pencil corrections or frowned when the wrong words were used. The daily practice of writing and reciting what were said to be true facts created strong reaction habits. Years later, people would answer "True" to statements they had been taught were true (such as "Grass is green"), even though they knew that grass is often brown in August (or when not watered), or blue in Kentucky.

So much for the language side of habit; now consider the emotional side. Getting cared for by our parents partly depended on using right words and avoiding wrong ones. Since we needed to be cared for in order to survive, words, especially wrong ones, took on an emotional significance far beyond their dictionary meaning. Perhaps you can recall when playmates felt hurt because they were scolded for using wrong words. Perhaps you can recall when playmates became angry because they were called names (wrong words).

As time passed, we went from elementary into middle school and beyond. We learned new words; we learned new ways of combining words; we learned new ways of writing and speaking. Though we became more educated, we continued to get into conflicts. We will continue to as long as we react to words as true or not true, right or wrong. You may protest that you know that things aren't necessarily black or white, that statements of fact (for example, "People can't be trusted") aren't wholly true or wholly false. What I am saying is that you can intellectually know that and still react in terms of right/wrong, perhaps without even realizing it. Of course, that's not true all the time; but if you're like most people, you have particular blind spots, words that arouse anger, anxiety, and other strong reactions. Your close friends and family members probably have a good idea of what those blind spots are, even it you don't. If you don't believe me, you might ask them.

What was drilled into us in our youth, what our parents gave and withheld affection for, what our teachers praised and scolded us for, does not disappear simply because we develop new learnings. Our emotional habits of reacting to others' words as being right or wrong remain with us, continue to plague our lives, and prevent us from attaining the quality of life we desire.

The emotional cost is high for believing that words are either true or not true representations of fact. The emotional cost is high for believing that people are wrong when they don't use the "right" words. We expect too much of our words. They can't accurately describe the complexities of life. We expect too much of the people who use them, and we are much too quick to judge people as being wrong simply because the words we hear are not the ones that we would have used.

The cost is also high in terms of money. Advertisers spend millions of dollars to advertise their products because they know that we will respond to their advertising as if it were the truth. They know that if they tell us that BLUE SOAP, for example, is sexy, we will buy BLUE SOAP. Millions of us will buy it.

For many reasons, responding to words as if they were facts (to be accepted or rejected) is a self-defeating act, one that gets us into trouble time and time again. Fortunately, there are alternatives, but to use them effectively we have to loosen the stranglehold that traditional language usage has on us. The next chapter moves in that direction.

CHAPTER 2

Freeing Ourselves From the Grip of Self-Defeating Habits

On one hand, there is a world filled with things, events, people, and wonders of nature. On the other hand, there is language, which can be used to describe that world and the experiences of the people in it.

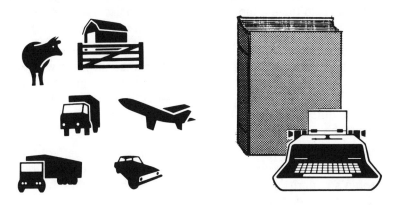

What relationship, if any, exists between the two? We'll begin to explore that question by contrasting winged, two-legged, feathered creatures that fly, with the words that people use to talk about them.

Habit: A Cause of Conflict

Somewhere out there, winged, two-legged creatures are flying. They have been flying for centuries (we assume). They were flying before man invented the word "bird" or created the names for different types or species of birds. These creatures continue their ways of flying whether or not the words "bird," "flying," "birds flying," or "birds not flying," are spoken. Using words from other languages, such as Swahili, Dutch, Malay, Portuguese or French, doesn't seem to affect these creatures, whether or not the words are used "correctly" or "incorrectly."

When we see these creatures flying, we could say, "Look at those catfish flying," and neither flying creatures nor fish creatures would change nor be any more pleased or offended than if we had said, "Look at the Glumfkx flying." And whether we spoke the words or wrote them down, whether we stated them as scientific truths or composed poems, whether we made up definitions or cited the results of research, none of that would make any difference to the flying creatures.

Just as creatures called birds go their own way regardless of the words we use, so do other living things and processes of nature. For the most part, we have given up the magical belief that words can affect nature, but we have not given up the belief that words can describe it accurately. One of our goals, of course, is to have a language that can precisely mirror nature. We have worked hard over the centuries to achieve that goal.

We now have common usage words, scientific words, slang words and words with different shades of meaning, and we have these in a variety of languages, We have words that are quite specific and words that are more general. We have developed better guidelines and customs for combining these words in ways that aid communication.

In spite of all that, our language still falls short of perfection in its capability to describe events. Can language describe a robin's pattern of flight? or a particular robin so that it can be distinguished from all other robins? Can language describe the taste of water? Can language describe the changes in the shape of the sea as the tides move in and out? Can language even come close to describing an evolving relationship between two people?

...and I thought I knew how to communicate!

And now let me remind readers that language does not speak, people do. The imperfect expressive capacity of language is further limited by the imperfections of the persons using it. Individuals have inadequacies of observation, interpretation, memory, knowledge, reasoning and vocabulary; individuals have hidden biases and motivations for speaking. My advice to listeners is: "Proceed with caution."

Don't assume that a speaker's words necessarily state the truth, the whole truth, and nothing but the truth about experience. Sometimes a speaker's words don't even come close. John told me, "All cows are born with three wheels, one eye, nine horns and a purple goatee. The wheels are of different sizes and the goatees change color from purple to green depending on the season of the year." As his listener, I found this statement interesting, literate and grammatically correct, but I did not assume that the words bore much resemblance to the truth.

Perhaps you have heard of the jackalope, an animal that roams the plains of Montana. I've seen one stuffed and mounted in a bar there. Its head is similar to that of a jack rabbit but with horns somewhat like those of an antelope. When I was in Montana, I was told that Easterners come to hunt them in the fall. While we're on the subject of hunting, would you be interested in going snipe hunting with me? I know where there are several herds. You'd find it quite exciting and on the way we pass by the field where the three-wheeled cows graze.

You who believe that words are closely tied to events in the world may feel that my examples (particularly my three-wheeled cow one) are unfair. I'll agree that words can come closer to depicting reality than some of my examples suggest. **How much closer, however, is a question to be raised rather than an assumption to be made.** The two basic points I want to make are, (I) that listeners have no guarantees that a speaker's words accurately fit corresponding events, things or people in the real world, and (2) even under the best of conditions, a knowledgeable person, who has the best of intentions, who is communicating the most accurate information and using appropriate words, can not consistently describe real world events with accuracy.

Consider, for example, the shape of the earth and our attempts to describe it by calling it "round." When we say "round," we are hiding the fact that there are hills, mountains of varying sizes and shapes, valleys, and flat but uneven surfaces like deserts. Furthermore, there are changing tides, shifting sands and volcanos—all working to change the shape of the earth, even as these words are written. Our experiences tell us that the shape of the earth is constantly changing. Thus, we know that the word "round" is but a rough approximation that overlooks irregularities, and is misleading in that "round" does not allude to the changing nature of the earth's surface. As this example and others to follow illustrate, the truth, the whole truth, and nothing but the truth, is extremely hard to put into words. A listener who believes otherwise is walking on slippery ground.

A different kind of truth-reporting problem comes about when we want to use words to distinguish one object from similar ones. Words are often inadequate for such a task. Consider what words we might use to distinguish one lemon from another in a sack of lemons. I've asked students to do that and they fail miserably. They can, however, distinguish one lemon from other lemons by touch (thus they find that there are differences among them). With their eyes closed, I ask the students to experience lemons by touching them. (The whole procedure is reported at the end of this chapter.) Eventually, individuals can tell their own lemons from as many as 20 others by touch, but not by words.

The distinguish-a-lemon-with-words problem may seem trivial to readers, but the students who experience the lemons usually don't see it that way. They get attached to their lemons and go so far as to refuse to give up their lemons to make lemonade. (And don't you get attached to your particular luggage, car, furniture, clothes, etc., so that it's important to you that each piece be distinguished from all others that are similar?)

"Lemon" and thousands of other words refer to any one of a number of things, people and events which are not exactly alike. Confusion often arises as to what in particular is being referred to. Does the word "fruit" refer to a tomato? If not, why not? (A tomato certainly has many of the characteristics of fruits.) Is commercial catsup a "vegetable"? Could an almost pure tomato catsup be considered thick "vegetable juice"? Is a "Bloody Mary" vegetable juice? At what particular percentage of fat, 2%, 1%, 1/2%, 1/4% is milk no longer called "milk"? In this book we're not really interested in these problems of definition. My point is that many words are vague and confusing as to what in particular they include and exclude. Words that are vague on this point lead to misunderstandings in which people mistake one meaning for another!

"I'd like a drink."

"Sure, I'll get one right away," I said.

"I wanted a drink, not water, stupid!"

A neighbor of mine had a dog that he said was friendly. A new family moved into the neighborhood. Their small son went down the walk to greet the friendly dog, only to be knocked down and have his face licked by the dog. The child's mother saw the incident and was furious. She ran to confront my neighbor: "I thought you said your dog was friendly."

"I did, and it is," my neighbor replied. "That dog was acting in a friendly way; he was trying to make friends with your son."

The child's mother replied, "Knocking kids down is not friendly. You keep that dog in your own yard!" And off she stormed.

As I analyze that interchange, each person had different meanings. For the mother, "friendly dog" referred to actions such as a dog wagging its tail and waiting to be petted. For my neighbor, "friendly dog" referred to actions such as a dog eagerly approaching children to play with them.

The word "friendly" does not have a good fit with a particular set of actions by dogs or people. Neither do words like lazy, smart, good, fair, unreliable, communist, democracy, love, honest, bargain, enough, soon, and a host of others. Listeners who assume they know which particular sets of actions are being referred to by words like that are heading for trouble.

Another problem with getting an exact fit between words and things is that things are continually changing over time, whereas words are fixed at the time they are thought or spoken. The result is that some descriptions, however accurate when they are initially formed, become less accurate as time goes by.

Native: It's low tide. You can walk all the way out to the island.

Visitor: Thanks for the tip. I'll get a few hours sleep and then go out.

Over time, words can become completely useless. Any of you who have acted on information based on observations made months earlier must know the hardship that results from slippage (over time) between words and what was observed.

I've tried to hammer home the point that words are not things. Words are not necessarily related to things. Words are quite often inadequate in describing one thing without including another that is not meant to be included. Words do not have the same qualities that things do. For example, the word "mushroom" does not taste the same as the soup which bears its name. Saying the word "mushroom" will not affect mushroom soup. Those are the main points. But to show you how completely we are hooked on the power of words, let me relate to you an incident that happened at my house.

At dinner one evening we were having a creamy thick soup. My son, who had commented that the soup was good and had eaten half the bowl, casually asked what kind of soup it was. Upon hearing the words "mushroom soup," he refused to eat any more and said the soup was "terrible."

That's really not much different than puckering one's mouth at the mention of the word "lemon," or reacting emotionally to words like "Negro," "Jew," "Catholic," "cancer," "communism," or becoming defensive when someone calls you names like "dumbbell," "ugly," "coward," "liar" or "stupid."

Even though we know that words are not the things, people and events they supposedly represent, we sometimes react to words as if they were. Even though we know that words do not correspond exactly to the things, people or events they supposedly refer to, we sometimes believe that we know exactly what is meant.

...and I thought I knew how to communicate!

There is a vast gulf between words and experiences, between the words that describe and the events that are being described. The bridge between is person-made. People are not always knowledgeable, not always reliable and not always motivated by the best intentions. They are forced to rely on a language system that is hopelessly inadequate for telling the exact truth, the whole truth, and nothing but the truth about life. Does that mean that no one or nothing is to be believed? Of course not. People can often convey enough truth about experience to be helpful. Words that are not totally accurate are still better than no words. What is needed is a change in the way we think of and use language. Tradition and habit have us do it their way, but there are other ways, ways that hold great promise for preventing misunderstanding and for building better relationships.

Skill Builders

2.1 Old Woman/Young Woman

Purpose:
To make you aware that what you see is not the same as what is there.

Directions:
Show this page to various people, one at a time. Ask them to tell you what they see. Make note of the facts they state. Ask enough people and you'll uncover two seemingly contradictory sets of "facts," one pertaining to a "young" woman and the other pertaining to an "old" one.

"Young woman" - what some people falsely assume to be fact: The "young woman's" face is seen in profile. She is facing left. Her face is white. All you can see of her face is her left cheek, left eyelash and tip of her nose. Her hair is black. She has a feather, which is just above and to the front of her head. You can see her left ear about the middle of the page. The left side of her long neck disappears into the mass of black that makes up the bottom part of the page.

"Old woman" - what some people falsely assume to be fact: The "old woman's" left eyelash is at about the center of the picture. Her left eye is the same as the younger woman's left ear. Her nose occupies the same area as the younger woman's left cheek. Her chin disappears into the black that makes up the lower part of the picture. She has black hair and a white shawl, which takes up most of the area in the upper right quadrant of the picture.

...and I thought I knew how to communicate!

A more accurate description of fact: The illustration on page 15 consists of black lines on a white surface. One continuous black line consists of straight edges and right angles so that it *appears* to form a border or frame. There are other patterns of black lines that *seem* to *suggest* faces and clothes. One of the faces *appears* to be that of a "younger" woman; another that of an "older" woman. The black lines can be *interpreted* in such a way that the young woman *appears* to have certain features and the old one certain other features.

Human beings are inclined to think that what they see is fact. Thus, they often make faulty assumptions about what the facts are. Can you see how a person who saw a young woman in the drawing could get into an argument with one who saw an old woman? That kind of interaction happens every day. Two people argue, both believing they know the truth but the other does not.

If you can remain aware of the distinction between personal viewpoints and things or events, then you can understand that other people might have different views than yours, even of the same observed set of facts; you can keep in mind that any further discussion you might have is about personal views, not facts. That kind of awareness can save you from getting involved in many nonproductive arguments.

2.2 Mental Maps Become Outdated

Purpose:
To demonstrate that mental maps become inaccurate over time.

Directions:
Recall that a few pages back I mentioned that a fundamental problem with the fit between words and events is that events change over time. Words that might have described well at one time may no longer be appropriate, and no one may realize that the words no longer fit.

Recall what your hometown was like as you grew up. Let yourself see the various streets. . . schools. . . people. . . pets. . . cars. . . yards. . . activities that were taking place. . . . See yourself alone. . . with friends. . . in the school room. . . on the playground. . . at home. . . in the morning. . . in the evening. . . .

Put these and other memories together and you have a map of your hometown as you knew it. . . . Allow yourself to realize that things have changed since then. Much of what you remember is different now. . . . You are not doing the same things you did, in the same places with the same people. . . . Your neighbors have grown older. . . . Your school has different children playing on the playground. . . . Your friends are doing different things. . . , cars. . . , streets. . . , pets. . . all have changed in some respects.

Because of changes that occur over time and because your mind does not accurately record all that happens, your present map in some respects is no longer a trustworthy map of your hometown. And you have no way of knowing for sure which parts of your map are relatively accurate and which ones are not.

For example, does your map include the names and faces of all the various persons who live in the nearby apartments, mobile homes or houses? Are these various neighbors in their dwellings right now? Are you sure? Where are your friends and acquaintances right now? What are they doing right now? Are you sure?

...and I thought I knew how to communicate!

Where do the people in your life hide the things they don't want others to find? Are you sure you know?

Your map of your current world is like your map of your hometown—incomplete and inaccurate in unknown ways—containing some "facts" that are no longer true. Right now, without your knowing it, a friend may have changed an attitude, a street crew started work, a car tire gone flat, a business address changed, an acquaintance taken ill. Even now something will be different than it was a few seconds ago. A car is several blocks further on its journey. A song on the radio is not on the same note . And so it goes, with people and events ever-changing, and you're stuck with a map that is not up to date.

2.3 Words Are Insufficient

Purpose:
To demonstrate that language is not precise enough to enable one person to accurately describe to another what is there.

Directions:
Below is a drawing. Look at it and describe it to other people. Ask them to reproduce the drawing from your verbal description (and without them seeing what you are describing). Compare their drawings to the one shown below. Are they alike?

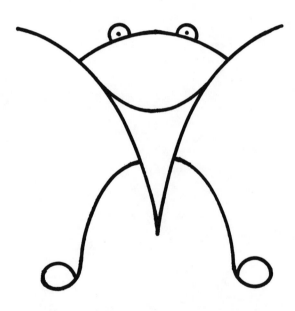

If you weren't completely successful, that doesn't mean that there is anything wrong with you, only that language doesn't do justice to what is.

...and I thought I knew how to communicate!

2.4 Family Picture

Purpose:
To help you to realize that people make erroneous conclusions about what they see.

Directions:
Ask someone to tell you what the facts are by completing the questionnaire on the following page.

Which of the following statements are true, false, or cannot be answered at all?

	(T)	(F)	(?)
1. The Jones Family owns a TV set	( )	( )	( )
2. Johnny is doing his homework while he watches TV	( )	( )	( )
3. Johnny's mother subscribes to a newspaper	( )	( )	( )
4. Mr. Jones is reading a book.........	( )	( )	( )
5. Mr. Jones is a non smoker	( )	( )	( )
6. There are three people in the room ..	( )	( )	( )
7. The Jones family subscribes to TIME and READER'S DIGEST	( )	( )	( )
8. The Jones family consists of Mr. Jones, Mrs. Jones and Johnny	( )	( )	( )
9. They have a dog for a pet	( )	( )	( )
10. They are watching an evening television show	( )	( )	( )

...and I thought I knew how to communicate!

NONE OF THE STATEMENTS CAN BE SAID TO BE TRUE FROM WHAT YOU ACTUALLY SEE IN THE PICTURE.

1. You do not know that the set is owned by them; it could be borrowed, or a demonstration set.
2. You do not know whether Johnny is doing homework or not; all you can see is that he has a book in front of him.
3. You do not know that Johnny's mother subscribes to a newspaper; you only know she is holding a newspaper. Matter of fact, you don't know she is Johnny's mother, either. She may be an aunt or friend just visiting in the house.
4. You do not know that it is Mr. Jones, and you cannot tell if he is reading the book he is holding.
5. You do not know that Mr. Jones (if, indeed, that is Mr. Jones) does not smoke. You only can see that there is a clean ashtray.
6. You do not know how many people might be in the room; you can only see that there are three people in the part of the room shown in the picture.
7. You do not know what magazines they subscribe to. The ones on the table may have been purchased at a newsstand or loaned by a friend.
8. You do not know if this is the Jones family; nor can you tell if there are other members of the family who are not present.
9. Could be a neighbor's dog, making itself at home.
10. You cannot tell if it is evening or not; only that the lights are on. Perhaps it is a cloudy weekend.

The typical person will answer "yes" or "no" to two-thirds to three-fourths of the questions. Given the true state of affairs, shouldn't you be a little cautious when responding to statements of fact such as "there are three people in the room," "They have a cat for a pet," "Johnny is doing his homework?"

Thanks to Don Fabun in *Communications* (see Postscript) for the idea.

2.5 Food for Thought and Discussion

Purpose:
To stimulate and clarify your thinking about relationships among words, people and events.

Directions:
Reflect on the following items.

I. What are some of the ways in which people develop false ideas about each other and about events in the world? Give examples.

2. What can people do to increase the accuracy of their understanding of each other and of events in the world?

3. People often talk to each other in language patterns that oversimplify or distort facts and result in misunderstandings. Give examples of these language patterns.

4. What ideas do you have as to how people can learn to accept each other's views of the world?

5. What can you do to decrease the number of false conclusions you make in forming ideas about other people and events in the world (for example, the types of conclusions you may have made in the previous Skill Builder)?

6. Often, arguments over so-called facts end up as struggles over who is right and who is wrong (as if words had to be judged in terms of right and wrong). Is there some way we can show disagreement without making others wrong? or without staunchly defending our own rightness (which has the effect of making others wrong)?

...and I thought I knew how to communicate!

2.6 Lemons Have Individuality

Purpose:
To demonstrate that people make important distinctions in life that they cannot put into words.

Directions:
Obtain as many lemons as there are individuals to participate (as many as 18 can easily be accommodated). Seat everyone in a circle. If people don't know each other, give them a chance to get acquainted. Then pass out the lemons. Ask the group members to pass around the lemons slowly in a clock-wise direction so that each person has a chance to see each lemon and to notice how one might differ from another.

After all have had a chance to see all the lemons, ask them to stop passing the lemons so that each person is left with one lemon. Move the chairs slightly so as to form small groups of three people each.

Ask them to stop talking.

Ask them to close their eyes. Allow a few minutes for them to settle down and become silent. Tell them: "Use this opportunity to touch, feel and otherwise experience the lemon you hold in your hand. Become aware of its unique characteristics. Please be silent so that you can concentrate on what you are doing."

After a few minutes, ask each group to rotate lemons clock-wise among themselves, still without talking, still with eyes closed. Ask them to become aware of how each lemon is different from the other two.

See that the lemons rotate slowly, allowing ample time for silent examination, until it seems apparent that individuals can tell their lemons from the others. Ask them to stop passing and to hold their original lemons. Then move the chairs so that two groups of three now form a group of six. Say, "Please remain silent and keep your eyes closed. Now pass the lemons clock-wise. Pass them until each one of you can tell your lemon from the other five. After you feel confident that you can do that, stop passing the lemons and keep your own."

Move chairs to re-form the original large group. Give the people a moment to renew acquaintanceship with their own lemons, then collect all the lemons. Randomly distribute the lemons, one to a person. Ask them to pass the lemons around the circle, slowly feeling each one. Say, "Continue passing until each of you recovers your own lemon." (As before, the passing should be done silently with eyes closed.)

As the group members find their own lemons, they should stop passing the lemons. Each person will then have a lemon. Many people, if not all, will have their original lemons and they will know that. The passing stops.

Have them open their eyes. You might ask how many believe they have their original lemons? How many are not sure?

Invite them to share feelings about their lemons and about the lemon-passing experience.

CHAPTER 3

An Alternative Way of Communicating
(That May Have Advantages)

In the diagram below, the various figures represent objects and their interrelationships. Between the objects and the dictionary is a space that depicts the idea that objects and words are not necessarily connected.

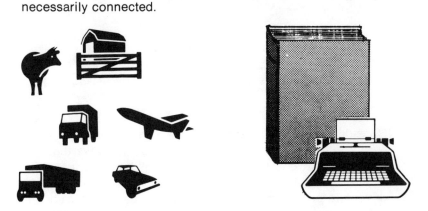

Connections are made when people use specific words to refer to corresponding objects, for example, when a reader used the word "white" to refer to this page.

Word/object connections are developed in a human process called meaning-making. That process begins with an act of perceiving closely followed by acts of thinking and reacting.

Meaning-Making process

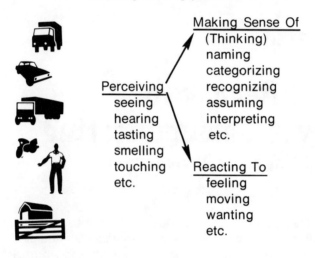

Perceiving
 seeing
 hearing
 tasting
 smelling
 touching
 etc.

Making Sense Of
(Thinking)
 naming
 categorizing
 recognizing
 assuming
 interpreting
 etc.

Reacting To
 feeling
 moving
 wanting
 etc.

Consider a meaning-maker, person A. Person A **sees** person B waving a hand in an up and down motion. A **thinks** that B is waving goodbye to a friend. A **feels** warmth and sadness. For another example, a driver **hears** a siren getting louder. The driver **interprets** that to mean that a police car, fire truck or ambulance is approaching. The driver **reacts** with excitement and **pulls over** to the curb.

...and I thought I knew how to communicate!

Meaning-making may occur in a different sequence than is depicted in the preceding diagram. ***Thoughts, beliefs and feelings, existing in the mind before perceiving takes place, influence perceiving.*** That's implied by the statement, "You only see what you believe." Whatever the sequence, the point remains that meanings belong to people, not to objects.

Meaning-making is often more elaborate than is suggested in the diagram. Concluding, remembering, generalizing, relating, planning, reasoning and other mental acts may take place. Eventually, some of the contents of the meaning-making process are selected and used to form the words and sentences of the speaker.

Meaning-Making Process

Perceiving

Making Sense Of

Reacting To

Elaborating Selecting

Objects

Words

As this diagram illustrates, any words that may be spoken are products of the speaker's meaning-making process. Such words may or may not have any connection with the objects to which they refer. If what is spoken does have a connection with the objects, that connection is a product of the speaker's mental process.

There appear to be objects in the world. The only way we can determine anything about them is through our senses and mental processes. Referring to objects, **speaking facts about objects, is basically a process of communicating select aspects of meaning that we believe reflect what we have perceived.** We can only report our meanings. We speak meanings, not facts.

Dialogue

TLU: (Traditional Language User) That's a good diagram and does illustrate that people get information through their eyes and ears. But aren't there some facts that everybody knows are fact? I mean like "old"; either a person is old or not old. Certainly no one would confuse a young baby and an old man as to which was old and which was young.

Author: Sure. I think we could agree that one was "young" and the other "old." As I see it though, our agreement is a matter of agreeing on particular words to talk about particular people. We can agree on words without having to believe that either "old" or "young" are basic properties of the persons we are talking about.

TLU: Look, a 75 year old man is old! There are no two ways about it.

Author: To you it seems that way. However, others might see that person differently. I had occasion to mention a family friend to my grandmother who was 90 years old. She replied, "Him old? He just retired, got a lot of life ahead." What one person views as old, another can view as not old. And that's not a problem when you consider that each of those words represents a personal meaning developed from an individual point of view.

TLU: What about young? Isn't it a fact that a day old baby is young?

Author: I can talk with you about a day old baby in those terms. No problem in that until we start believing that young is a quality of babies. If it were a quality, then it

...and I thought I knew how to communicate!

should be relatively easy to determine which babies are young and which are not. Suppose, for example, you were telling me about the young babies in a children's ward in which there were many children ranging from newborn up into the teens. If I went there looking for the young babies, how would I know which specific ones, from the many of different sizes, ages and shapes, you were talking about?

TLU: I'm not sure.

Author: Then I question whether "young" is a fact about babies or a word idea attached by people with their own personal meanings in mind. Let's explore that idea further by looking at the young baby problem from the younger side of young. When young babies are younger, say in their mothers' wombs during the ninth month of pregnancy, are they young babies? young something elses? or by virtue of the fact that they are younger, are they actually old fetuses? or what? Is whatever it is a human being? If so, at what earlier point is it not a human being? Many factions of society—politicians, mothers, physicians, scientists, religious leaders, philosophers, lawyers—are now wrestling with those questions. If you have a definite answer, be clear that it is an opinion (not fact); your opinion will probably conflict with others whose opinions are just as firm as yours might be. In areas like this, there may be facts, but all we have are personal meanings.

TLU: I'll try once more. Look at that thermometer. It reads 86 degrees. Now that is a fact, right?

Author: It looks to me like it's near 86 degrees also. But I'm reluctant to say that the temperature is 86 degrees. It's not likely to be exactly 86 even if it looks that way to us. And for all we know, that particular thermometer might be in error; 85 or 87 degrees might be more accurate. More importantly, the warmth of nature does not come naturally packaged in degrees. We don't see the warmth of nature at all.

	What we see are man-made lines calibrated to certain man-made numbers beside a column of mercury.
TLU:	It seems to me that you're being picky about words. Whether it is exactly 86 or not doesn't make any difference.
Author:	It isn't the numbers I'm being picky about. I'm objecting to the belief that what we see exactly duplicates what is. I'm objecting to the belief that there is only one way of seeing things. You are right in terms of your own meanings. I hope I've made it clear that I agree with you on that. The problem comes about when you try to make your meanings universal truths; that's when we differ.
TLU:	It's hard to let go of the idea that one's words do not speak truth.
Author:	I know how you feel about that. It's hard for me too. I look at your picture on the wall and the word "weird" pops into my mind. That word and the meanings that accompany it are in my mind even as I first look at the picture; the word and the picture almost seem to be part of the same substance and thus the word seems true of the picture. If you were to comment that your picture was creative, my impulse would be to say that you were wrong and to think you had bad judgment because it seems so obvious to me that the picture is "weird," not "creative." To avoid thinking you're wrong, I have to remember that it was me who put the word "weird" in my mind. I have to remember that you're looking at your picture from your viewpoint, not mine, and that it is only natural that you would use a different word to refer to it than I would.
TLU:	I feel very uncomfortable giving up the certainty that grass is green, water is wet, and my picture is creative. I want to hang on to and defend such statements; they seem so true, but I'm willing to listen. What's next?

Translate Words as Meanings (Not Facts)

Speaker's
Objects➤Meaning-Mak-➤Speaker's ➤ Listener
ing Process   Words

From a listener's perspective, it makes sense to assume that a speaker's words are based on that speaker's meaning-making process, and that a statement of fact is actually a disguised statement of speaker meaning. ***When another person speaks to you of facts, you (as listener) could translate that person's words into perceptions, thoughts, feelings and other aspects of meaning.*** For example, if a good friend said to you that his girl friend was unfaithful, you could translate what you heard and say to him, "You've heard some things about her," or "You've started to have some doubts about your relationship." If a neighbor said that Chicago was a crummy place to live, you could translate and reply, "You don't like being there," or "It doesn't seem to you to be a good place to live."

When translating facts into meanings, communicate what you consider the most important meanings to be. Because your understanding of these may not be exactly what the speaker intended, translate tentatively, look and listen for clues from the speaker that confirm or clarify your translation. If you wish, you can always ask for confirmation, for example, "Is that what you mean?"

When translating, do it in the spirit that speakers' meanings are real for them, that from their standpoints their meanings are supportable, believable and contain some truth. In an earlier example, a friend said, "My girl friend is unfaithful." A reply, "You've seen her do some things that make you wonder about your relationship with her," is more supportive of your friend than is, "You only think she's unfaithful."

When translating, do the best you can without worrying unduly as to whether or not you're right. If you're a little off the mark, your speaker will likely clarify and continue. For example, your friend might say, "I haven't actually seen anything myself, but I've heard some stories about her." Through that clarification, you'll have a clearer picture of what your speaker meant, and your speaker will know that you've been paying attention and trying to understand.

Advantages of the Meaning-Making Approach

We were taught that there are facts in the world; indeed there are. Put some apples on a table and most people will agree that there is a flat surface with four legs (what we call a table) and round, red or green (yellow too) edible objects (what we call apples).

We were taught that there are verbal statements that describe facts in the world. There are verbal statements of fact but these can't be counted on in the way that we have been taught to believe. In a previous chapter, I mentioned a so-called fact, " The world is round." How can that be a true statement when we know that the world is flat in places, mountainous in places and continually changing shape!

Consider "2+2 = 4." I could take two apples and add them to two more apples and we could count four apples. That would seem to make "2+2 = 4" a true statement of fact. Then I could take two cups of milk powder and add it to two cups of water, and after stirring, end up with something less than three cups of liquid. It seems that the so-called facts "2+2 = 4," "The world is round" and so on are not exactly true in the way we have been taught.

The problem is not with nature but with words and the ways we traditionally use them. The word "is," for example, speaks to existence. If something exists, "It is." If it doesn't exist, the statement "It is" is said to be false, because something can't both exist and not exist at the same time. This use of language leads to problems. If someone says that "John is lazy," our traditional view of language holds that he either is or he isn't lazy, that he can't be both or neither. In reacting to the statement of fact "John is lazy," a listener's training pushes that listener toward agreeing or disagreeing. If a listener agrees, that solidifies a false picture (that John is always lazy and never exhibits any degree of not-lazy, that laziness is a quality of John and is therefore deemed to be resistant to change). If a listener disagrees, that listener is likely to be involved in an argument over whether John is or is not lazy.

From the meaning-making perspective, neither false agreement nor disagreement need occur. A speaker says, "John is lazy." A listener translates and replies, "He appears lazy to you."

Speaker: He sure does. He sits around and doesn't do a damn thing about getting a job.

Listener: I take it then that you'd like to see him get a job, and the sooner the better.

Speaker: That's right. I work for a living and I hate freeloaders.

(Note that "appears" and "you'd like" both refer to speaker meanings.)

Statements presented as fact, such as "John is lazy" or "Taxes are too high," are the stuff out of which conflicts develop. People who make statements of fact usually have good reason to believe that their facts are true. Therefore, they tend to react defensively when listeners say they are not. Sooner or later, a listener will disagree, "What do you mean too high? It costs money to pay for police protection, good schools and garbage disposal services. If we want services, we have to pay for them." Listeners who disagree have good reason to believe that what they say is true. They, too, naturally tend to defend their positions. With the kind of language used in such a dialogue, one person has to be right and the other then has to be wrong, and of course, nobody really wants to be wrong. Arguments develop and friction follows.

In the meaning-making approach no argument need ensue, even when the listener disagrees (holds a different point of view).

Speaker: Taxes are too high.

Listener: (translates) Possibly you're going to have to pay more than you think you should.

Speaker: That's right. Last year taxes were $900; this year they jumped to $1,200.

Listener: (translates) And you don't think that increase is justified.

Speaker: No, I don't. I think it's unfair.

Listener: (quits translating and presents own view) I don't know if you know this, but the police, firefighters and garbage collectors all got pretty hefty raises this year. I believe some increase is justified.

The sharing of views continues.

In summary: Apparent statements of fact, such as "Women are terrible drivers," tend to push listeners toward agreement or disagreement. Agreement strengthens a misleading view of the world and perpetuates false beliefs (all women are terrible drivers under all conditions and will never be anything else). Disagreement fails to acknowledge what is true (a few women are sometimes less than excellent drivers), and often leads to tension in relationships. In the meaning-making approach, neither conflict nor false agreement need ensue; working relationships may be maintained while individual meanings are shared. The facts that underlie those meanings may be clarified to the benefit of both parties.

Speaker: Women are terrible drivers.

Listener: (translates) Apparently you've had some problems with cars driven by women.

Speaker: Right on!

Listener: (asking for speaker's perception of facts) What happened?

After speaker provides perception of facts, listener can relate her own experiences if that seems warranted. After that, they can continue to explore similarities and differences in their respective experiences and possibly come up with a statement with which they can both agree.

...and I thought I knew how to communicate!

Other Advantages to a Meaning-Making Approach

A listener's translation provides a speaker with immediate feedback as to what the speaker's communication means to the listener. This helps the communication stay focused and prevents misunderstandings that result when people don't connect with each other or misinterpret what is said.

When listeners realize that statements of derogatory facts are disguised speaker-meanings, those listeners can translate the so-called facts as speaker-meanings and keep themselves from becoming unduly upset.

Speaker: You never listen to me!

Listener: (reminds self that speaker's words are about speaker's meanings, not facts about the listener) You seem angry with me about something.

Considerations

Communicating translations of meaning, even when they are accurate, can cause problems. People expect other people to view language in the ways they have been taught to view it. Consider a statement in which, from the speaker's point of view, the facts are clear cut, "My roof is leaking." For a listener to say, "You've seen water dripping and you interpret that to mean your roof is leaking" would likely antagonize the speaker (even though that is probably what really happened). For the speaker, the leaky roof is 100% fact. However, certainty is misplaced here because there is a chance that the speaker's roof no longer leaks or has been fixed (assuming the observation was made earlier and the roof is not visible at the moment the statement is made). Nevertheless, it may not be smart for a listener to convert facts into something less solid by referring to them as thoughts or feelings, or by repeating what seems to be obvious.

You can think meaning-making without actually communicating your translations. You can think meaning-making while responding in more conventional ways; for example, "How did it happen?" or "What did you do?" In general, the further a speaker gets from obvious facts, the greater the need for the meaning-making approach and the less chance that a listener will rub the speaker that wrong way.

If you have an on-going relationship with someone and you start to respond to that person in new and different ways, you can expect to get curious glances or comments, even resistance or hostility. The person may be caught unaware and at a loss to know what your purpose is. If you've newly begun to translate and resistance arises, I suggest that you tell the other person what you are doing. For example, you might say, "Sometimes you state things as facts that seem to me to be more like beliefs or thoughts. That's why I substituted 'You believe' for 'It is.'" For example, you might say, "I said what I did because I want to keep our discussion focused on our wants, thoughts and viewpoints instead of getting into a conflict over who's right and who's wrong." Another option for you is to share, in advance, the meaning-making idea with others so that they can understand what you're doing and why you're doing it.

Although translation of fact into meaning provides a breakthrough in many situations, it is only one of many types of response a listener can make. At times, other types of responses described in the following chapters may be more appropriate.

A Comparison of Traditional and Meaning-Making Responses

To close this chapter, I'll reproduce some statements of fact I've heard speakers make. These are followed by listener responses in the traditional mode (agreeing, disagreeing and I know what you mean) and then by listener responses that employ the translation-to-meaning approach. Notice how listener translations give speakers the opportunities to explain further what they mean. Speakers tend to appreciate such listeners. Also, notice how listener translations preserve opportunities for continuing communication and exploration of meanings without introducing argument or false agreement. That's usually a plus.

(A) Politician: Communists are trying to undermine our economy.

Traditional Responses:

You bet they are.
You don't know what you're talking about.
I know what you mean.

Meaning-Making Translations:

You believe strongly that communists are a threat to us.
You've heard some things that give you cause to be concerned.
There may be some truth to what you way. What, in particular,
do you have in mind?

(B) Best friend: (angrily) You're no friend of mine. You've been
spreading rumors behind my back. (Assume
listener is not sure what this is all about.)

Traditional Responses:

You're nuts.
Who's been feeding you those lies?
How can you say that after all we've been through?

Meaning-Making Translations:

You must have heard something that offended you. What is it?
You seem pretty upset with me.

(C) Neighbor: You can't trust people these days.

Traditional Responses:

They'll rip you off every time.
That's really not true.
I know what you mean.

Meaning-Making Translations:

Apparently you've lost your faith in people.
You're afraid to trust anyone.
You're not sure whom you can trust these days.

You may not think that the meaning-making responses I have
given are the best responses that could be made. I'm not sure
they are either, but they do offer alternatives. And we'll be considering still other alternatives in the chapters to come. This
book is about choices, not about prescriptions.

Advice From a Confirmed Meaning-Maker

— Don't assume that you know what someone else means.
— Don't take words, your own or other people's, to be facts about the world.
— People don't speak facts; they speak meanings.
— Don't reject or doubt people simply because the words they use seem to be factually incorrect.
— Do accept words as a means for you to get closer to whatever facts you are interested in obtaining. When facts are important, ask for the speaker's perceptions.
— Do consider words to be expressions of personal meaning and vehicles which you can use to build relationships with others. (More on that in the next chapter.)

Skill Builders

Chapter 3: AN ALTERNATIVE WAY OF COMMUNICATING (THAT MAY HAVE ADVANTAGES)

3.1 One Fact: Multiple Meanings

Purpose:
To show how different people develop different meanings relative to the same fact.

Directions:
People develop meanings for themselves on the basis of what they perceive, coupled with whatever expectations, beliefs, emotional reactions and other meanings they bring to bear on a situation. Each person is different. Thus it is likely that different people will develop different meanings even when perceiving the same event. Relative to the following situation, develop a possible set of meanings for each person.

Situation: Sally brought home a report card on which the letter "B" appeared as her grade in Social Studies. Sally hadn't studied very hard and had been half afraid that she might get a "C."

Sally: When she saw the "B" she felt _____ . She thought _____. She had an urge to _____.

Sally's mother: Sally's mother liked to brag about the scholastic successes of her children. Sally's older sister had earned all "A's." When Sally's mother saw the "B," she felt _____. She thought_____. She had an urge to_____.

Sally's brother: Sally's brother was often compared to Sally. If she earned higher grades, especially if she got "A's," he often was scolded for not being as bright. When he saw Sally's "B," he felt _____. He thought _____. He had an urge to _____.

Sally's friend: Sally's friend, Mary, had worked harder than Sally, so Mary thought she would get a better grade than Sally. Mary received a "C." When Mary saw Sally's "B" she felt _____. She thought _____. She had an urge to _____.

Meaning is personal; keep that in mind.

3.2 Listening for Personal Meanings

Purpose:
To practice translating stated facts into personal meaning equivalents.

Directions:
Below are six speaker communications. Following each are blank lines. On those lines write translations of personal meanings to communicate to those speakers.

1. **Teenage boy:** School is a drag! All day we sit and listen to this boring stuff that doesn't mean anything. What use is knowing parts of speech and junk like that? Summer can't come too soon for me.

   _____

   _____

   _____

2. **Teenage girl:** Boys are jerks! They're more interested in watching that stupid TV sports stuff than they are in talking or doing stuff with girls. And they're so immature! They could be late for a date simply because some football game went into overtime!

   _____

   _____

   _____

3. **Father:** What's with kids these days! They don't seem interested in learning skills. They don't appreciate the value of education and they won't save money. What's going to happen when they have to make their own way in the world?

   _____

   _____

   _____

4. **Neighbor:** Work is for the birds! _____

   _____

   _____

...and I thought I knew how to communicate!

5. **Young adult:** My brother has been getting into all kinds of trouble. He'll end up in jail if he doesn't take it easy.

_____

_____

_____

6. **Friend:** You've been telling stories behind my back!

_____

_____

_____

My Translations (not necessarily the best)
1. I get it that you're bored with school and believe that some of the subjects, especially English, won't be useful to you.
2. You've had some negative experiences with boys who seem to you to be overly involved with sports.
3. I understand you to mean that many kids don't seem to you to be serious about preparing for adult work and that you're concerned about what may happen to them.
4. As I get it, you're fed up with your job.
5. You seem to be quite concerned about your brother.
6. You believe that I've somehow done something to hurt you.

Don't be concerned if your translations are not exactly like mine. If yours include "you" or "yours," have at least one word that refers to personal meaning, and show acceptance of what the speaker said, pat yourself on the back for getting the idea.

3.3 Practicing Listening/Translating Skills

Purpose:

To provide an opportunity for you to practice the oral translation of stated facts into personal-meaning equivalents.

Directions:

You'll need a partner who will talk about some aspect of life. While that person is talking, you'll be listening. Don't worry about what you're going to say or do next. Let yourself be open to receive what the other communicates. Your listening task is to understand your partner's personal meanings and to then communicate your translations of those meanings to your partner.

Orient your body for attentive listening by facing your partner squarely. With head tilted forward to aid listening, and with eyes on your partner, say, "I'd like to hear about something that interests you." As your partner speaks, encourage with head nods and appropriate words. After a paragraph's worth of meaning has passed and there is a pause, communicate your translation of personal meaning, then indicate with your eyes or by gesture that you want the speaker to go on. Be open to what your speaker says in reply. If you didn't catch your speaker's meanings, the speaker will probably let you know right away and then you'll both be clear as to what the conversation is all about.

Continue to listen attentively, offering visual and vocal encouragement as the speaker continues. After another paragraph or so, again communicate your translation of meaning, encouraging the speaker to go on after you do so.

Continue this speaking/listening/communication process for one or two more interchanges; then summarize to the speaker all that has been communicated in terms of the speaker's personal meanings.

Ask the speaker to confirm, clarify, correct or elaborate on the various aspects of your summary.

Ask the speaker to comment on how it felt to be listened to. What did your speaker particularly like about how you listened? Comment on your experience as a listener.

It would give you valuable additional practice if you would repeat this exercise with another speaker.

...and I thought I knew how to communicate!

3.4 Listening While Arguing

Purpose:

To practice the oral translation of facts into meanings under difficult conditions while taking opposing sides in a discussion.

Directions:

Obtain a partner. Select a topic about which the two of you have differences of opinion. Discuss that topic in two different ways.

First, each of you counter with your own ideas every chance you get, interrupting, asking pointed questions, and presenting your opinions with little regard for the other's position. After a few minutes stop your discussion and share your feelings about what happened.

Second, each of you allow the other to continue talking until the other pauses to get a response from you. Then, before you express the points you wish to make, put into your own words (translate) the main points of what you heard your partner say. The pattern to follow is: one person speaks; other translates message, then expresses self; first speaker translates that, then expresses self; other translates that, then expresses self. Continue that pattern for as long as either of you has something additional to say.

After your discussion is completed, share your feelings about what happened during the second process as compared with the first.

3.5 Barriers to Listening

Purpose:
To identify your internal barriers to effective listening.

Directions:
In the preceding activity you probably became aware that (1) the presence of your own thoughts and images prevents you from hearing others, and (2) your reactions to other people color and interfere with your hearing what they have to say. Make a list of the kinds of thoughts, images and reactions you have that seem to interfere with your being a really good listener.

3.6 Increasing Listening Effectiveness

Purpose:
To expand your ability to listen effectively.

Directions:
Being a good listener is necessary if you really want to understand another person's meanings fully. The following exercise helps you to develop your listening capabilities. You'll need a partner for this. Face your partner squarely in a comfortable position with no barriers between you. Ask your partner to read this activity silently and quickly, then to read these instructions aloud to you. (If a number of people are doing this activity at the same time, it is better if one person reads the instructions slowly aloud for all listeners like yourself to hear. Partners wait silently until it is time for them to speak.) When reading the instructions aloud, allow five seconds to go by at each series of dots.

...and I thought I knew how to communicate!

Relax. . . . Close your eyes, let your breathing come slowly and naturally. . . . Focus your attention on your breathing. . . . Let go any tensions you may be experiencing in your legs. . . in your arms. . . in your shoulders. . . in your neck. . . in your face and head. . . . You are now more relaxed. Let go any other tensions you still have and focus on your breathing. . . . In your mind's eye you see a blackboard (pause). As a thought passes through your mind, let it appear on the blackboard and then disappear. . . . Watch this process as it continues. A thought appears on the black board and then disappears. . . . Notice that your mind is emptying itself of thoughts, that your thoughts are coming more slowly. . . (read more slowly) and are slowing down. . . . Your thoughts have quieted down now. . . . Keep watching the blackboard and if any further thoughts come, let them appear and then disappear. . . . Let any remaining tension disappear. . . . Focus on your breathing. You don't need to make a favorable impression on anyone. You are not responsible for helping me (your partner). Soon you will be listening to me (your partner). All you need to do is listen (pause). All you want to do is listen (pause). Allow yourself to be open to what you see and hear. Even though your eyes stay closed, get an image of your eyes opening wider (pause), get an image of your ears opening wider and deeper (pause). Inwardly you are now more open and more receptive and more available to me (your partner). Perhaps you can imagine that your ears are opening like funnels (pause). You are able to hear a great deal because your ears are wide open (pause), and now (and in a louder voice) open your eyes so that they too are open (pause). Let any tension go. . . . Remain relaxed. Now tilt your head forward slightly so that you are looking at me (your partner). Wait silently and listen. I (your partner) will now speak.

Tell your listener what you've been thinking, feeling, seeing, imagining, etc. during the last ten minutes. Continue to relate your experiences for at least three minutes. Then say to your partner, "Tell me what you understand of what I have just communicated." When your listener has finished, either confirm, clarify or add to listener's understanding.

Listener: Tell speaker what your experience as a listener was.

Repeat activity with a new speaker.

An Alternative to Communicating

3.7 Food for Thought and Discussion

Purpose:
To sharpen personal viewpoints on understanding people by challenging and discussing stated guidelines.

Directions:
In this chapter a number of statements have been made that provide guidelines for listening in a meaningful way. These statements are neither wholly true nor false but more or less true depending on which particular set of facts one has in mind. Some of the more important statements are presented below. Discuss them with other people in an effort to determine their usefulness in various circumstances.

Don't assume that you know what someone else means.

Don't take words, your own or other people's, to be facts about the world.

People don't speak facts, they speak meanings.

Don't reject or doubt people, simply because the words they use seem to you to be factually incorrect.

Do accept words as having possible connections with facts. Perceptions, yours or others, are as close as you can get.

Do consider words to be expressions of personal meaning. Accept them as meanings, even though you may have different perceptions of the facts and doubt that the other person's version is accurate.

...and I thought I knew how to communicate!

CHAPTER 4

Sometimes Words Don't Count:

Feelings are Expressed Nonverbally

In previous chapters the emphasis has been on listening to words. The emphasis now shifts to listening to vocal sounds (such as sobs, pitch, intensity, loudness and inflections) and watching for patterns of physical movement (such as gestures, facial expressions and posture). These provide important clues as to how persons are feeling. To understand feelings, it is necessary to notice and translate nonverbal clues.

Physical Expressions of Feelings

If you saw a person sitting all alone, head hanging down and crying, it wouldn't take much imagination to realize that person was feeling sad. Similarly, if you saw a man, fist raised and tightly clenched and pounding the air with his fist as he chased another man, you would guess that the man who was doing the chasing was angry.

In neither of these examples were any words spoken. The physical expressions of the persons told their stories. When people are caught up in emotions and feelings, physical signs are clearly visible. But not all feelings are as easy to read as the examples I've cited here.

Vocal Expressions of Feelings

A shriek of terror, a mother's sobbing at the death of her child, a joyful cry of greeting, the sound of a familiar voice over the telephone, these too communicate feelings. I recall a time when my brother and I were playing in the living room. We heard my mother, who was in the kitchen, calling his name, nothing else. My brother's comment was, "She's annoyed at something. I better go see." And away he went. He got his feeling clues from the way her voice sounded.

Acknowledging What is There

To some of you, these examples may seem so obvious that you're wondering why I'm making a big deal of them. I'll tell you why. In my experience, people are apt to respond out of habit and fail to recognize the obvious, or recognizing it, fail to communicate that recognition.

Jill listens; her mother talks, "It would be nice if you called your Aunt Sarah. She's always been so kind to you, and it is her birthday." There is an accusatory ring to her voice. Jill replies, "Alright, Mother." Had Jill communicated the obvious, she might have said, "I hear an edge in your voice that leads me to believe you're disappointed in me."

Jim is talking with a friend. The friend's facial expression changes slightly and her head and shoulders move back an inch or two. Jim keeps on talking and then changes the subject. Had Jim communicated the obvious, he might have said, "I notice that you're reacting differently now and I wonder what that means."

Communicating what is clearly visible and audible provides an opportunity for what is below the surface to emerge, be clarified and subsequently dealt with.

A Perspective on Feeling

Throughout history, people have noticed that they were affected inwardly by things, events and people in the environment. To describe these inner experiences, they coined words like "feeling" and "emotional reaction." They also coined more specific words like "anger," "fear," "disgust," and "happiness" to distinguish one kind of affecting experience (feeling) from another.

Feeling words refer to changes in the body's pattern of functioning and to urges to react (move). In sadness, persons may experience lumps in the throat, sobbing, tears, a loss of energy and an urge to withdraw. In anger, persons may experience tension (often in the hands and face), a rapid increase in energy and an urge to do away with the object of their anger. In anxiety, persons may experience physical jitters, butterflies in their stomachs, rapid breathing and a strong urge to flee.

The basic physiological changes that occur in feeling experiences influence vocal sound and physical movement. Spoken words, when one is relaxed and breathing slowly, sound differently from when one is breathing rapidly (as in fear or excitement). Facial expressions, when one's facial muscles are contorted in anger, are different from when one is relaxed and happy. Eye movements, gestures, posture, body movements, rate of speech, loudness of voice, rhythm of words, pitch of voice and inflections are all influenced by the "feeling" condition of the body that initiates them. Shifts in these expressive features are detectable to any person open to hearing and seeing them.

Vocal sounds and physical expressions provide important clues as to what a given person may be feeling at any given moment. These clues are especially important when the spoken words do not include an appropriate reference to underlying feelings. A man says, "I'm really glad to see you. Sit down and let's talk." His voice sounds hurried and he glances quickly at the door from time to time. In contrast to the content of his words, his vocal and physical expressions point more toward nervousness than to joy.

Unfortunately, there is no good dictionary capable of defining which particular patterns of sound or physical expression mean which particular feeling. It's true there are many popular books on body language which purport to do that, but I encourage readers to consider these with a bit of healthy skepticism. There may be a few predictable patterns that fit everyone, but there will also be countless individual variations, some of which will be neglected by or even at odds with the published guidelines.

Translating vocal sounds and physical expressions into feelings becomes less difficult when one thinks in terms of families of feelings, each urging movement in different directions. Identifying the right family or families may be all that is needed to get the translation process started.

Feeling Families

Urge to Move Against (Anger)

Feelings in this family urge action against some person or thing, for example by taking, pushing aside, or eliminating. Anger, hate, irritation, annoyance, jealousy and envy are some of the names for urges of this kind.

Moving-against feelings are likely to be manifested by cutting remarks, "put downs," sarcasm, loud voices, increased muscle tension, gestures directed toward the object of anger, and increased levels of energy to be used for action.

Urge to Move Away From (Fear)

Fear is the key to this family. Apprehension, tension, anxiety, avoidance and nervousness are related. The resultant urge is to run away, avoid or flee from contact with the source of the threat. Fear and anger are similar in that both generate urges to move. People can easily tell them apart, however, because the movement in fear is away from; the movement in anger is against.

Urge to Move Toward (Love/Happiness)

In this family many of the same physiological changes as in fear and anger are present—more rapid breathing, increased energy and an urge to move. In this instance, however, the urge is to move toward, rather than away from or against. Movements in facial muscles and gestures also differ. Enough about that. I'm sure that you're all capable of detecting the difference between love and fear or love and anger.

Urge to Withdraw (Sadness)

Persons who are sad, discouraged, depressed or gloomy lose the energy to move in any direction. Often, they feel tired. They may have the urge to cry. Their voices may sound different because they have been crying or trying to hold back tears; their voices may also be softer. They may be reluctant to say anything unless given a great deal of encouragement. They may lose interest in eating, working, and seeing other people. Their thoughts often turn inward.

Competing Urges to Act (Mixed Feelings)

Some, perhaps most, feelings involve two or more different urges to act. Feeling angry at someone you love is an example. In such cases, affected persons might say they felt torn, undecided, upset or pulled in two different directions. They might actually move from one urge to the other (for example, toward the telephone to make a call and then hanging up the receiver before they dial). Feeling words, like "jealous," "hurt," "bitter," and "disappointed," often describe two different families, though in a way that is not as clear cut as the love/anger example. Sometimes, feeling words refer to affecting conditions in which one feeling, such as sadness, gets partially substituted for another, such as anger, so that a mixture of the two remain (and one urge covers over another).

Translating Sound and Movement as Feeling

Even simple feelings have many dimensions, including (a) *perceptions* of what was reacted to, (b) *physiological sensations*, (c) *thoughts* about the cause or object of the feeling, (d) one or more *urges to act*, and (e) *second thoughts*. This example illustrates. Peter is walking by a restaurant with his brother when he (a) *sees* his steady girlfriend go into the restaurant with another man; (b) his *muscles* in his arms, trunk and throat *become tense*; (c) he *thinks* that she is stepping out on him; (d) he has *an urge* to run into the restaurant and drag her out; (e) he *thinks that this might not be the smart thing to do.*

Although the whole person, in this case Peter, is involved in the feeling, not much of the feeling appears on the surface. What can be seen and heard—a sudden shocked look of recognition, clenched fist and jaw and an exclamation—is just enough to indicate that feelings are present; a feeling translation is in order.

For the brother, one possibility is simply to tell Peter what he sees and hears, for example, "Your jaw is clenched," or "Your voice sounds angry." This recognition encourages Peter to bring more of his feeling into the open. As he does, his brother can translate other aspects as they emerge, for example, "You think that she's unfaithful," or "You feel like dragging her away." ("You feel like" is another way of saying "You have the urge to.")

When you translate what you see and hear, use words that are appropriate to the level of intensity of the feeling expressed and to the lifestyle vocabulary you both tend to use. After translating, pause, look and listen for confirmation or further elaboration.

Sometimes you are the perceived cause or the object of the speaker's feeling. The speaker says to you (with glaring eyes and angry voice): "You idiot!" You can translate that feeling statement just as you might any other: "I get it that you're mad at me"; pause, look and listen.

Translating into Feeling Words: Some Examples

In these examples, use your imagination to hear the voice and see the physical expressions of the speaker, since I can't provide these in this written text.

Example A

Person 1: (sitting by herself with body drooping and downcast eyes).

Person 2: (translates) You seem sad (or) You feel like being by yourself (pauses, looks and listens).

Example B

Person 1: That dirty slob of a roommate ran off with my stereo and owes me 25 bucks. No way to know where he is either. What a rat he turned out to be. (Voice is loud, intense, "pointed"; facial expression is tense, eyes narrowed; right hand clenched in a fist is gesturing toward the door.)

Person 2: (translating into feeling) You're angry at your roommate because he ripped you off (pauses, looks and listens).

Example C

Person 1: Ever since he told my brother that he's gonna get me, I take a different route home each day and lock all the doors and windows at night. (Voice is quiet, as if not wanting to be overheard; eyes glance all around, as if on guard.)

Person 2: (translating into feeling) It's kind of scary for you when you think about what he might do (or) You have the urge to hide (pause, looks and listens).

As I mentioned earlier there are probably not as many pure feelings as there are those with mixed elements. The following examples illustrate the latter.

Example D

Person 1: I do want to get married. John and I have been going together for a long time and we really hit it off, like being on cloud 9, (pause) but I've put off naming the wedding date once. I'm thinking about putting it off again.

Person 2: (translating into feeling) I get the idea that you're really in love with John, but also a bit scared of actually making a commitment to him (pauses, looks and listens).

Example E

Person 1: I've got a couple of friends that haven't got any more on the ball than I have. And yet they seem to get the breaks, so that both have good jobs and happy marriages. I'm stuck with a wife that doesn't love me and a dead-end job. It's not fair.

Person 2: (translating into feeling) You sound like you're a little jealous of your two friends and angry as well— perhaps with yourself, or with other people who haven't given you what you think you deserve.

Apparent questions can be translated as feelings. The vocal sounds and the patterns of physical movement that accompany the speakers' questions provide the material for translating.

Example F

Person 1: Where were you last night? (loud intense voice).

Person 2: (translating into feeling) You're mad at me, is that it?

In our society, many of us have been taught to cover up feelings. For example, a man might hide the fact that he's sad or afraid. A woman might hide the fact that she's angry or frustrated. In such cases, voice and physical activity often give messages that conflict with the messages in the spoken words. When that happens, consider translating words, vocal sounds and physical expressions separately. In the following example, Person 2 does this.

Example G

Person 1: No, I am not angry! What makes you think I'm angry? Why should I be angry? Speech is rapid, voice loud, body tense, face tense, and finger pointing (as if to accuse).

Person 2: You sound to me like you're angry at someone; your words say you're not. I'm confused.

Reluctant to Translate?

I've found that some people are reluctant to communicate translations of feelings, because they don't want to "label" another person falsely. What if you say to another person, "You sound upset," and that person is not really upset at all? My reply is that if you come across as being interested in that other person, as being friendly and helpful, warm and involved, then that other person is not likely to feel labeled or accused. Getting a specific word or words wrong isn't likely to ruin things. The purpose of communicating translations of feeling is not to label anyone, the purpose is to speak in a way that can facilitate communication of feelings and related meanings. The urge of emotional arousal is to let energy out; a listener who can help with the letting-it-out process can solidify a relationship, remove a source of friction and be a better friend. Many times when communicating translations I haven't used the "right" feeling word. Perhaps I've said, "You sound irritated," when instead the other person felt disgusted. What often happens in such cases is that the other person may say, for example, "I'm not irritated, but I am disgusted," then continue telling me about personal feelings and related meanings. The fact that I didn't have the right word was not critical. The fact that I encouraged feeling talk was.

Closing Remarks

When feelings are disguised as facts, it is important to identify and facilitate their expression as feelings. The urge to act plays a key role in feeling. Recognition of that is vital.

There are times when translating feelings is probably not appropriate, for example, when you don't have the time or energy to follow through, or when the focus is on determining facts (such as is true with detectives, lawyers and doctors). There are other times, important times, when translating feelings is likely to be productive. Consider translating when:

—You want to develop or open up a relationship.

—You sense that a person's words aren't communicating the true nature of that speaker's feelings.

—You want to help a person deal with a problem or concern.

—You sense that there is a conflict or barrier between you and another person.

—You want to be clearer about the meaning of a message. (For example, you observe that a friend is agitated; you suspect your friend is angry, but you can't tell if the anger is directed at you or someone else.)

Feelings can get quite complicated so it may take a great deal of patience and practice to clarify and separate competing urges to act from each other or from thoughts and sensations, but it is often worth the effort. Whatever is meaningful in life involves feeling. Bringing feelings to the surface helps to keep your interactions on a meaningful level.

Skill Builders

Chapter 4: SOMETIMES WORDS DON'T COUNT: FEELINGS ARE EXPRESSED NONVERBALLY

...and I thought I knew how to communicate!

4.1 Tuning in to the Vocal Dimension

Purpose:
To sensitize yourself to messages conveyed in vocal sounds.

Directions:
Find a partner for this exercise. Read the exercise, then both of you close your eyes and talk to each other. Talk about something that you are interested in or concerned about. As you talk, each of you should be listening to the sound of both voices. After you have talked for a few minutes, keeping your eyes closed, tell the other person how that person's voice sounded to you and how your voice sounded to yourself. Ask your partner to do the same for you.

Keeping your eyes closed, change your topic of conversation and resume talking, again listening to both voices. Share what the voices sounded like to each of you. Comment about the congruency between words and sounds. If you were aware of any discrepancy between verbal and vocal messages, describe it.

Open your eyes and discuss your experience of the exercise.

4.2 Feeling Messages in Vocal Sounds

Purpose:
To focus on the expression and identification of feelings expressed in vocal sounds.

Directions:
Some of the feelings that people frequently express include anger, frustration, disappointment, nervousness, contentment, fear, excitement and detachment. These are conveyed, at times, in the vocal dimension. Obtain a partner. Tell your partner that you are going to convey one of these feelings. Don't give any verbal clues. Don't use words that name a feeling. Say to your partner, "Close your eyes," then find a way to express the feeling vocally. For example, you might say, "That stupid car of mine won't start again!" in a way that expresses frustration. Have your partner tell you what feeling you expressed and what the vocal clues were.

Reverse roles. Have your partner express a feeling while you listen with your eyes closed and attempt to name the feeling. Continue to reverse roles, expressing different feelings each time. It makes the game more interesting when one of the rules is that you can repeat (using different words) any of the feelings that were previously expressed.

Discuss similarities and differences you noticed as you interpreted feelings in each other's voices.

...and I thought I knew how to communicate!

4.3 Feeling Messages in Physical Activity

Purpose:
To focus on the expression and identification of feelings expressed through gesture, facial expression and other physical activity.

Directions:
Form a group of two to eight persons (4-6 is optimal). Below is a list of feelings that people often experience. One person should select one of the feelings to enact and write down the name of that feeling on a piece of paper without revealing it to the others. That person then expresses the feeling without using any sounds or words. In communicating the feeling, the expressor may feel free to move around, involve other players, use facial expressions or hands or any other nonverbal means.

After the expression, the others independently write down the name of the feeling and the urge to act they thought were being expressed. Afterwards the group members read what they have written.

List of Feelings:

> anger
> sadness
> happiness
> contentment
> loneliness
> excitement
> fear
> nervousness
> boredom
> love
> disgust
> annoyance

1. If at least half of the group has written down the name of the feeling word that the expressor communicated, it means that the feeling was successfully expressed. All who answered similarly, including the expressor, get one point. All others (those who named other feelings) get zero.

2. If at least half of the group has not written down the name of the feeling that the expressor communicated, that means the expressor did not succeed in communicating that feeling. In this case the expressor subtracts one point. Everyone else's point count remains the same. After points have been tallied, the person to the expressor's left writes down the name of a feeling that person is going to express; the process starts over again.

There are no limitations on which feelings may be expressed as the game continues. However, when a feeling is enacted a second time, the enactment must be different.

Each person is to get three turns. The one or ones with the most points at the end wins. The prize is some form of attention from each of the others (hug, massage, compliment, etc.)

...and I thought I knew how to communicate!

4.4 Translating Communication into Feeling

Purpose:
To practice the translation of factual communication into feeling terms.

Directions:
Below are three examples of speaker messages that I have translated into feelings. Following these are eight messages that you can translate. In each case, imagine that you are that speaker's listener and write in how you would translate that speaker's feelings.

Examples:

1. ***Parent:*** Get away from that paint! Johnny, I've told you before and I'll tell you again, GET AWAY FROM THAT PAINT!

   Listener (the other parent reflecting feelings) replies: You feel angry at Johnny (pause).

2. ***Mother:*** I've tried to get Marie on the phone three times today and every time it's busy. What's going on over there?

   Listener (a friend reflecting feelings) replies: I get it that you're pretty frustrated with trying to reach Marie (pause).

3. ***Boy:*** No, you didn't hurt my feelings. It's all right (and he sits in silence).

   Listener (his girl reflecting feelings) replies: From your silence I get the impression that you're probably a little irritated with me (pause). (Another possibility for her is): I hear your words about "not being hurt," yet by your silence I can't help thinking that maybe you are a little hurt by what I said (pause).

Now it is your turn to write responses. Don't be concerned that you might not get the feeling exactly right. Your response has nothing to do with being wrong, it has to do with your understanding of feelings. (You are the best authority on your understanding.)

1. **Wife:** The bread didn't turn out. The washing machine overflowed. The baby got his new clothes all muddy. I didn't get anything done all day. No matter what I tried, nothing went right!
   You (as her husband) reply: _____

   _____

2. **Brother:** You forgot to pick up my clothes at the cleaners. You never think of me, do you? (Remember, the focus is on the speaker's feelings.)
   You (as his brother) reply: _____

   _____

3. **Worker:** I really wanted to go to that game and I counted on you to be able to work for me so I could go!
   You (as fellow worker) reply: _____

   _____

4. **Wife:** You go out and play golf every Saturday and have a good time and leave me here. Then I sit all day with nothing to do and no one to do anything with. Saturday's are terrible!
   You (as her husband) reply: _____

   _____

5. **Friend:** I'm going to Europe this summer and for three months too!
   You (as friend) reply: _____

   _____

6. **Student:** I'm really looking forward to going to college next fall. I'll probably meet some neat people and take some interesting courses but I'll have to leave my boyfriend here and won't see him for a month, at least. That's a bummer! (Keep in mind that a person can have two feelings.)
   You (as listener) reply: _____

   _____

...and I thought I knew how to communicate!

7. *Girl* (after her boyfriend has forgotten to pick her up but later shows up with a plea to be forgiven): How do I know I can trust you?
   You (as boyfriend) reply: _____

   _____

8. *Friend:* I wanted to go on that trip so bad. I would have too, but then Tom called and asked me to go to the rock concert. He turned out to be a real dud.
   You (as friend) reply: _____

   _____

You can compare your responses with those of the author's. The author's responses (not necessarily the best) to the eight speaker messages are:
   1. *Me* (as husband): You sound pretty discouraged at all the things that went wrong today.
   2. *Me* (as brother): I get it that you're irritated with me for not picking up your clothes.
   3. *Me* (as fellow worker): I imagine that you're really disappointed with me because you didn't get to go to the game.
   4. *Me* (as husband): Apparently you're angry with me for leaving you alone Saturday.
   5. *Me* (as friend): You feel excited about your trip.
   6. *Me* (as listener): Sounds like you're having mixed feelings. You're enthusiastic about going to college but sad about leaving your boyfriend.
   7. *Me* (as boyfriend): You sound angry with me.
   8. *Me* (as friend): You're disappointed in Tom and in missing the concert.

Before you leave this activity, identify the urges to act that underline each of the eight speaker messages.

4.5 Nonverbal Characteristics of Feelings

Purpose:
To help individuals identify nonverbal expressions of feelings.

Directions:
On the chart below, in the first column, write down the name of a feeling you have experienced. Recall a time when you felt that way. Re-enact that feeling in front of a mirror or with the help of a friend. Identify the sounds in your voice and your facial expressions, gestures and physical movements that seem to express the feeling you are re-enacting. In the second and third columns, write down the vocal and physical signs of that feeling.

Continue repeating the process with other feelings.

After you finish, get together with other persons to discuss your understanding of what signs are visible and audible with various kinds of feelings.

COLUMN ONE Name of Feeling	COLUMN TWO What Your Voice Sounds Like	COLUMN THREE How You Appear

...and I thought I knew how to communicate!

4.6 Food for Thought and Discussion

Purpose:
To stimulate and clarify your understanding of feelings.

Directions:
Give some thought to the following questions as you reflect back on the material in this chapter.

1. How useful do you think feelings are? Do they seem to serve some useful purpose or do they seem to foul things up? Should they be encouraged to emerge or should they be controlled or hidden?

2. What should you do when someone you're talking to is angry at another person? What should you do when someone you're talking to is angry at you?

3. Do people ever cover up anger, sadness, fear or happiness? (Give specific examples.) How do cover-ups come across to others?

4. Discuss various mixtures of feelings, including feelings about feelings (for example, feeling angry because you're sad or feeling guilty because you're angry). How can another person best respond to someone who seems to be expressing mixtures of feelings?

5. Earlier in this chapter there was a list of five situations in which translation of feeling was said to be appropriate. Think about or discuss these situations with others. Do you agree or disagree?

4.7 Developing an Appropriate Feeling Word Vocabulary

Purpose:

To expand your vocabulary of feeling words and to learn to use words appropriate to the intensity of a particular feeling.

Directions:

In translating into feelings, it helps to have a variety of feeling words at your disposal to allow you to reflect different types and intensities of feelings. Below are the names of feeling families. Under each, list a number of different words, poetic phrases, slang expressions and so on that relate to that feeling. After you have ten to twelve words and phrases in a list, rank them in order of intensity. If you wish, share your list with others and get their reactions.

Happiness	Anger	Fear	Sadness

...and I thought I knew how to communicate!

4.8 Responding to Feelings in Real Life

Purpose:
To use imagery, to practice responding to the feelings of those who matter to you.

Directions:
Think of people with whom you have significant relationships. Think about how they communicate feelings. Imagine how you might translate their communications as feelings. Imagine one of these persons speaking as that person usually speaks. Now imagine yourself responding, but responding with a translation of feeling instead of responding from habit. Imagine how that person might respond to your translation. Imagine how you could translate that.

...and I thought I knew how to communicate!

CHAPTER 5

Intention:
Source and Purpose for Communicating

A big man in working clothes opened the door, called out greet-ings to several of the customers and sat down beside me at the counter. He turned to the man on the other side of him and asked (in a voice loud enough for the waitress to hear), "When are they going to get some decent help around here?" She came by and replied, "as soon as they get some first-class customers!" Several customers laughed.

Man: What kind of pies don't you have?

Waitress: If you want it, we don't have it.

Man: You don't have fresh peach, right?

Waitress: Right!

Man: Gimme a piece of fresh peach.

Waitress: (puts an empty plate in front of him) Here you are.

Man: I'm hungry enough for two pieces today. I'll take that moldy looking red one (pointing to a cherry pie).

Waitress: (hands it to him) Good choice. I've been trying to get rid of it for days.

Man: I believe you. Have you got a dust cloth? And what are these tire marks on top?

Waitress: You won't find anything dirty on top. When it fell on the floor yesterday, we turned it over on the plate so the top side is real clean.

Man: I don't doubt it at all. . . I'll need something strong to hide the taste. I'll need some of that battery acid you call coffee. One of these days the Feds are going to get you for false advertising.

Waitress: (brings cup of coffee) Hope you choke on it (and moves to another customer).

They exchanged a few more remarks that I can't recall. After ten minutes or so he paid the bill and left a tip on the counter.

Man: Bye bye piano legs; see you tomorrow (as he moves toward the door of the cafe).

Waitress: Don't you wish you were man enough to play the piano.

I had the idea that this interaction, with somewhat different dialogue, was repeated nearly every weekday afternoon. The other customers who had momentarily interrupted their own conversations to enjoy this little scene resumed their talking as I left the cafe and hurried to my car to write down the dialogue.

All indications were that the customer and the waitress had communicated effectively. They sounded friendly; they made contact, they conducted their business in a satisfactory way, said their goodbyes and left each other, apparently on good terms. Taking their words seriously isn't likely to help us understand the success of their communication; focusing on their intentions might. Intentions have to do with achieving desired goals. Assume that the man's goal was to play with the waitress in a friendly way. Assume that she had interpreted his communication correctly and that she had similar intentions in regard to him. Following through on their intentions they communicated playfully, in ways that aided the achievement of their mutual goals.

...and I thought I knew how to communicate!

Intention

Intending involves the transforming of a want (need, desire) into actions focused on obtaining a wanted (needed, desired) result. Suppose that I became aware that I want to pass an examination. I intend to pass it. I channel my energy into action and communication that will help me pass. I study. I read. I ask questions. I consult with others. I review my notes. My activity is purposefully guided by my intention to pass that examination.

With intention, it's not what words mean, not how voices sound, not how physical activity looks, it's getting desired results that count. A car salesman's communication can be understood more readily by realizing his intention is to sell a car rather than to provide information about the car (although information might be provided). A stranger's reference to the weather can be understood more readily by realizing that her intention is to engage in friendly conversation rather than to forecast the weather (although forecasts about the weather might be made).

The problem for potential listener/translators is that others don't always speak their intentions openly. Randy says to Sue, "What's our homework for tonight?" (His intention, not stated, is to spend time with her.) A mother says to her son, "Stay away from the quarry! You can't go swimming there!" (Her intention, not stated, is to keep her son out of danger.)

Though intention may not be openly stated, listeners can assume that it probably is present. The question is: "What does this person want to accomplish for self, with me, and with others?"

Translating Communication as Intention

Guidelines:

1. Listen to the content of the words. Consider the situation. Tune in to intensity, inflection and other vocal messages. Look at what the person is doing (face, gestures and body movements).

2. Imagine what the aims of your speaker's communication might be.

3. Check out the accuracy of one of your imagined aims. One possibility is to ask the speaker. (Do you want? Do you intend to? Are you going to? etc.) A word of caution: People sometimes hide or disguise their intentions so that you may have to decide whether or not their answers are truly reflective of their aims. Another possibility is to respond in a way that follows through on one of the hunches you have about your speaker's aims, then use your speaker's reaction to help you decide whether you're on the right track. Suppose for example, your speaker said, "That's easy; let me show you," then took over your task and completed it. Suppose that your hunch was that the speaker's intention was to impress you. You could respond, "You're pretty good at this aren't you." If the speaker's face "lit up" or otherwise showed signs of satisfaction, you could feel more confident that you knew what the speaker's aims were in regard to you. On the other hand, if the reply was "Not really, you looked like you needed help," you could feel more confident that the speaker's intentions were to be friendly towards you.

As a second example, suppose that one of your fellow workers is complaining to you about another worker whose sloppy work affects the complainer. You might guess that the speaker wants the other worker to get on the ball and do better work, but what does the speaker want from you, if anything? You could check that out by asking, "Are you thinking that I should do something about it?" The speaker's answer may clarify what the intention was in communicating this complaint to you.

Trying Your Hand at Translating Into Intention

Below is a list of twelve speaker expressions that convey intention and a list of twelve speaker intentions. Imagine appropriate vocal sounds and physical activities to accompany them. In the blank beside each expression, put the letter of the intention that you believe might lie behind it.

Speaker Expression | Speaker Intentions

1. ____Would you like a ticket to the game?   a. to persuade
2. ____My car makes a good buy for someone.   b. to reject
3. ____You lied to me.   c. to conceal
4. ____I know how to do it.   d. to work
5. ____Silence.   e. to defend
6. ____Go on.   f. to be friendly
7. ____Everybody will be there.   g. to understand
8. ____I never said that.   h. to avoid further contact
9. ____I realize that you're in a delicate spot.   i. to make a favorable impression
10. ____I'm sorry I didn't call you.   j. to obtain money
11. ____I've got to go now.   k. to mend a broken friendship
12. ____It's one o'clock. Lunch time is over.   l. to encourage

Here are my hunches as to what those speakers might have intended.

l. f, 2. j, 3. b, 4. i, 5. c, 6. l, 7. a, 8. e, 9. g, 10. k, 11. h, 12. d.

You may not have the same answers I do; your's might be better, who knows? Take the next step by thinking what you might say, to each of those speakers, to check out your hunches. I'll give two examples to illustrate. Speaker 10 said, "I'm sorry I didn't call you." I took that to mean that the speaker wanted to make amends and move closer to me (k). To check that out, I might say, "Go ahead. I'm listening."

As you think of ways to check out your hunches, keep in mind that speakers may deny intentions that they don't want revealed. When you suspect that might be the case, check out your hunch indirectly. One way is to encourage the speaker to say or do something else that provides you with additional information about a particular intention. My next example illustrates this. Speaker 11 said, "I have to go now." Thinking she may want to avoid further contact (h), I might ask, "Will you be calling me later?" and listen for traces of warmth or coldness in her voice as she answers.

It's your turn. How might you check out your hunch about number 1 and the rest?

Multiple Intentions

In the previous section, communications were translated in terms of speakers' intentions toward listeners. Speakers' intentions also relate to themselves and to people other than listeners. With that in mind let's examine number 12, "It's one o'clock. Lunch time is over." Several workers are eating lunch together. Possibly the speaker intends (1) to go back to work and intends (2) to let the listeners know that is why the speaker is leaving. (The speaker doesn't want them to take the leaving as an unfriendly act.) Another possibility is that the speaker wants (1) to make a favorable impression on the boss and wants (2) to keep the listeners from being late and getting into trouble. A third possibility is that the speaker wants (1) to leave to avoid dealing with a particular topic and wants (2) to conceal that intention from the co-workers.

Though it is not always easy to translate intention, if you don't somehow identify and address your speaker's needs/wants/desires, misunderstanding will likely result. On the other hand, misunderstanding may result if you assume that you know what is in someone else's mind. For example, I heard a neighbor say (with certainty in his voice), "She deliberately was late, just to spite me." I knew that he and his wife were having problems, and I couldn't help but wonder if his tendency to jump to conclusions about her had anything to do with their splitting up.

My suggestion is to make tentative translations and then check them out. In that checking out process you will gain additional information that will either strengthen your impression or lead you to another possibility. Fortunately, it isn't often that you have to act on the basis of a single communication. With people with whom you have repeated contacts, you usually get several opportunities over time, to check out the accuracy of your translations.

Verbal, Vocal and Physical Expressions of Intentions

At times, people notice discrepancies between what is verbally and physically expressed. Friend No. 1 says to friend No. 2, "I'd like to get together with you again. I'll call you one of these days." Weeks go by and the call doesn't materialize. The physical expression of an intention (in not-calling) apparently contradicts the verbally expressed one ("I'll call you"). With intentions, actions speak louder than words. What I mean is that intention is energy directed at satisfying a want. The absence of energy directed toward calling is likely to be a better clue to the strength of an intention than are the words, "I'll call you." But one can't be sure of that. Friend No. 1 may really·want to contact friend No. 2, but other wants may be more urgent at the time. It would be desirable for friend No. 2 to get further information before coming to any firm conclusions. The problem with translating intention is complicated by the fact that there are many wants and feelings which energize and urge people in various ways.

Sorting out Intention

As indicated in previous chapters, our feelings are triggered by persons and objects as we try to reach our goals. Barriers to finishing work appear and we get angry or frustrated; a person who means possible trouble calls and we get nervous; someone we love arrives unexpectedly and we feel happy. And so it goes. Feelings produce urges to move—in anger we move against, in fear we move away from, in love we move towards, and so forth. On the surface, these urges to move are similar to the urges to move initiated by intention, but there are important differences. *Feelings are the results of reactions to events and produce movement that relates to those events. Intentions are created by self and produce movement that fulfills a want/need/desire of self.* Feelings and intentions co-exist, sometimes masking or conflicting with each other, as the following example illustrates.

Tom said, "Sometimes I feel like belting my two sons. They take my tools and then don't return them, and maybe leave them outside in the rain or something like that. I want to teach them a lesson. I'm sick and tired of not being able to find my tools when I need them, and I'm concerned that my sons aren't learning to respect other people's property. I think that's important, and I think that maybe if I punish them hard enough that they'll soon get the message. But I don't like the idea of hitting children."

Is Tom propelled by feelings? By intentions? By both? Let's try to sort it out. It seems to me he is initially expressing a feeling (anger), a reaction to his sons' behavior. Underneath, it seems to me that he has intentions that run in a different direction (thus causing a conflict). Tom wants to have his tools available and in good condition when he uses them. He wants his sons to grow up to be responsible and to learn to take care of tools properly. He wants to accomplish all of this by acting in a manner he believes is appropriate. His intentions push him in one direction. Along the way he gets thwarted by what his sons do. As a reaction to being thwarted, his anger urges him to act against his sons.

...and I thought I knew how to communicate!

If I were to translate Tom's communication, sorting out these various elements in the process, I would probably say something like this: "Tom, as I get it, you want your tools to be in good shape and available when needed. You want your sons to respect other people's property and to grow up to be responsible adults. At the moment you're angry at them because they're not acting in a way that satisfies either of your wants, and you want to figure out how you can accomplish all of this without resorting to physical force." And if Tom were talking to me, I would add, "My guess is that you want me to help you figure out how you can do that."

To some readers my translations may seem to take a risky leap from what Tom said. Yes, there is risk; there is always risk of error in making something clear that initially was ambiguous. I believe, however, that the possible gains for both of us in clarifying the nature of his concerns is worth that risk.

Summary

Intentions of speakers may be buried, but be assured that they exist. Because intentions are often important (as in the customer/waitress example), try to identify them and to separate each one from various feelings and conflicts that also motivate people. In doing this you can build a more solid base of information upon which to base your own responses or actions and you can be in a better position to help others get more of what they want in life.

The separation of feelings from intentions can be very important when you are dealing with someone you might want to help (as with Tom). This separation is crucial when you are dealing with a person with whom you have a mutually caring relationship. Sometimes that person may get angry, irritated or frustrated at something you did, yet still care for you. As you hear the communication you may only hear the anger and assume that the person no longer cares, when in fact the caring is still there even though covered over with anger. Consider that anger may not be that person's basic intention toward you. Allow that person to express the anger, so that you can better understand more of the underlying personal meanings. Maybe you can see how caring still exists, even though anger is being expressed. If in this process you communicate caring, it may be possible for the other's caring to surface.

Skill Builders

**Chapter 5: INTENTION: SOURCE AND PURPOSE
FOR COMMUNICATING**

...and I thought I knew how to communicate!

5.1 Conveying Intention Messages Nonverbally

Purpose:
To focus on the expression and identification of intention.

Directions:
For this activity, you will need a partner. If you can form groups of four to five, that would be ideal.

Below is a list of intentions:

to care	to ignore	to avoid
to be polite while not really caring	to defend self	to persuade
	to be right	to advise
to be unfriendly	to conceal	to be humble
to impress	to please	to dominate
to flatter	to play	to be dominated
to understand	to fail	to take risks
to support		to play it safe

Let a member of your group be the speaker. That person selects one of the above intentions and attempts to convey it (in whatever ways seem appropriate). The speaker tries to convey the intention either directly to the group members or to an imaginary person while the group observes. The observers then state which intention they thought the speaker was conveying as well as what they saw or heard that led them to form their impressions. Group members should try to understand how each other's impressions were formed.

Rotate so that one of the other group members becomes the speaker. Continue the process until each member has had an opportunity to convey three intentions.

Discuss the following questions:

1. What is it that makes an intention come across clearly as opposed to being vague or confusing? (Be as specific as possible in answering.)
2. To what extent do listeners use the speaker's words to decide what the speaker's intentions are?
3. How do people ignore, conceal, distort or falsify their intentions?
4. To what extent are people usually aware of their intentions as they speak?
5. Why don't people usually name their intentions directly as they speak?

Intention: Source and Purpose for Communicating   81

5.2 Separating Intention from Feeling

Purpose:
To identify the different intentions and feelings of characters in a mini-drama.

Directions:
In the following story, there are four people. For each, write down your best hunch as to what that person was feeling, and your best hunch as to what that person intended. (Remember that it is commonplace to have more than one feeling and one intention.)

Father is reading the newspaper. Mike and Jake come into the room arguing over whether Jake ruined the plug to Mike's electronic game. Mike is loudly accusing Jake. Jake denies that he is to blame. Mike says to Father, "Make him buy me a new one. He ruined it and it's his fault." Jake protests that it was an accident, that the cord was left where anyone could trip over it. Father yells, "Get out. Settle it yourselves. If you can't, I'll help after supper. Now get going." As soon as the two leave, Mother comes in from the kitchen and scolds Father, "You shouldn't be so harsh on them!"

Father wants (for self): _____

Father wants (for Mike and Jake): _____

Father feels (as a reaction to Mike and Jake): _____

Mike wants (for self): _____

Mike wants (Father to): _____

Mike feels (as a reaction to his father's yelling): _____

Mike feels (as a reaction to Jake's ruining the plug): _____

Mother wants (for self): _____

Mother wants (Father to): _____

Mother feels (as a reaction to Father's yelling): _____

Mother feels (as a reaction to Mike and Jake's fighting): ____

Mother wants (Mike and Jake to): _____

...and I thought I knew how to communicate!

Jake feels (as a reaction to Mike's accusation):_____

Jake wants (Father to):_____

Jake wants (Mike to):_____

My guess is that Father is angry or annoyed with Mike and Jake. He wants peace and quiet for himself; he wants them to go away. Mike wants a new plug; he may want Father to punish Jake or he may want Father to see that he, Mike, gets a new plug. Mother is irritated or annoyed with Father for yelling and with Mike and Jake for fighting. She wants Father to be more patient with the boys and wants Mike and Jake to be mature enough to settle their differences. Jake feels angry at Mike for putting all the blame on him. Jake wants Father to see his side of the story and not make him buy a new plug. Jake wants Mike to quit picking on him.

I'm not saying my interpretation of this scenario is the right one. If you don't agree with me, talk it over with someone else; see what the two of you can agree on. Actually, it's not agreement but the sorting out process that's important.

Take a few minutes to think back to a recent situation in which you were interacting with people who are close to you, then try to sort out the various forces that were affecting you all (much as was suggested in this exercise).

5.3 Watching/Listening for Intentions

Purpose:
To practice the tentative translation of nonverbal activity into intention terms.

Directions:
Write in two translations of intention that you believe might underlie each of the following communications. (I'll do the first one as an example.)

1. Speaker: offers you a drink on a hot summer day.

My translations: wants to be friendly; wants to be thought of as a thoughtful person.

2. Speaker: after exchanging a few remarks, mention that there is a good movie this week at the local theater.

Your translations: ⎯⎯⎯⎯⎯⎯⎯⎯⎯⎯⎯⎯⎯⎯

⎯⎯⎯⎯⎯⎯⎯⎯⎯⎯⎯⎯⎯⎯

⎯⎯⎯⎯⎯⎯⎯⎯⎯⎯⎯⎯⎯⎯

3. Speaker: starts to talk before you have completed your story.

Your translations: ⎯⎯⎯⎯⎯⎯⎯⎯⎯⎯⎯⎯⎯⎯

⎯⎯⎯⎯⎯⎯⎯⎯⎯⎯⎯⎯⎯⎯

⎯⎯⎯⎯⎯⎯⎯⎯⎯⎯⎯⎯⎯⎯

4. Speaker: asks a number of questions about a mutual friend.

Your translations: ⎯⎯⎯⎯⎯⎯⎯⎯⎯⎯⎯⎯⎯⎯

⎯⎯⎯⎯⎯⎯⎯⎯⎯⎯⎯⎯⎯⎯

⎯⎯⎯⎯⎯⎯⎯⎯⎯⎯⎯⎯⎯⎯

5. Speaker: apologizes for an unkind remark made a few days ago.

Your translations: ⎯⎯⎯⎯⎯⎯⎯⎯⎯⎯⎯⎯⎯⎯

⎯⎯⎯⎯⎯⎯⎯⎯⎯⎯⎯⎯⎯⎯

⎯⎯⎯⎯⎯⎯⎯⎯⎯⎯⎯⎯⎯⎯

...and I thought I knew how to communicate!

6. Speaker: complains that you are driving too fast.

Your translations: _____

_____

7. Speaker: doesn't answer the telephone when you call
(you know he is home).

Your translations: _____

_____

8. Speaker: holds out a sack of popcorn in your
direction.

Your translations: _____

_____

9. Speaker: asks you about class assignments for
several days in a row.

Your translations: _____

_____

10. Speaker: asks you for a map of Chicago.

Your translations: _____

_____

11. Speaker: mentions that his girlfriend or wife is out of
town.

Your translations: _____

_____

_____

12. Speaker: tells you that her mother is a famous doctor.

Your translations: _____

_____

_____

5.4 Recognizing Verbal Intention Statements

Purpose:
To sharpen your ability to distinguish between intention statements and some look-alikes.

Directions:
In each of the situations below, there are three alternative responses. Put a check beside the one that most clearly states the speaker's intentions.

1. Mr. Dewberry has a new saleslady working for him in his store. He notices that she seems to be talking a lot with the other salespersons so that customers are not getting waited on promptly. Mr. Dewberry (speaking to new saleslady):
   a. You've got to talk less with the others and wait on customers promptly, otherwise I'll be forced to let you go.
   b. One of the rules is no socializing on the job. From now on, you are to follow the rule, understand?
   c. I want to tell you that I've been aware that you are not waiting on customers as rapidly as you could. I'd like to keep you employed here, but that will partly depend on how effectively and promptly you wait on our customers.

2. Bob has been working as an electrician's helper. His boss bawled him out one day when Bob wasn't doing what he had been told to do. Bob (speaking to his boss):
   a. It's not my fault. Nobody ever told me how to do it.
   b. Please show me how. I want to learn to do it right.
   c. What is this Pick on Bob day? I'm not perfect you know..

...and I thought I knew how to communicate!

3. Jane has been looking for her jacket, which she believes she put in her closet. She asks her mother where it is. Her mother replies that she saw it yesterday in the TV room. Jane yells angrily back at her mother that she doesn't leave jackets lying around. Mother (speaking to Jane):
   a. Well it doesn't have legs to move itself. It's where you left it.
   b. If you put your clothes away more often you wouldn't have this problem.
   c. I suggest you look in the TV room. I'd like to help you find your jacket.

4. Jim's girl friend, Sue, gives him a cashmere sweater for his birthday, but it is too big for him. Sue feels sad about this. Jim (speaking to Sue):
   a. Maybe I'll grow into it. I could wear a turtle neck underneath; that would work out fine.
   b. It's a nice sweater. I like it and I'll take it back and exchange it.
   c. It's not your fault, Sue. How could you know that the clerk put the wrong size in the box!

5. Jill, Mary's roommate, has a habit of not doing the dishes promptly when it is her turn. Mary is then faced with fixing the next meal without counter space or clean dishes. Mary likes Jill. Mary (speaking to Jill):
   a. I want to work out an arrangement with you. I'd like to have clean dishes and counter space available when I fix dinner for us.
   b. (Mary doesn't say anything to Jill about the dishes because she doesn't want to hurt her feelings.)
   c. You're terrible about doing the dishes. Here are yesterday's dishes still in the sink.

5.5 Food for Thought and Discussion

Purpose:
To resolve the dilemma of choosing between pursuit of desired goals and feelings toward others.

Directions:
People have intentions to reach goals that are meaningful to them. In pursuit of their goals they encounter and interact with a variety of other people, who evoke feelings of various kinds and intensities. People then have the choice (theoretically at least) of either continuing toward their initial goals or following the urges of their feelings. This dilemma seems to underlie many stories in which work conflicts with play, commitment with romantic attraction, relationship with career and saving for the future with impulsive spending.

When should we put aside feeling urges to move on toward our goals? Develop different perspectives on this, rather than thinking solely in terms of should versus shouldn't. To make your thoughts or discussion more concrete, talk in terms of specific situations, for example, infatuation versus career commitment, or saving for a future dream versus buying something that attracts you now.

5.6 Self-Awareness of Intentions

Purpose:
To increase your awareness of your intentions and how you express them.

Directions:
Place a check mark in the appropriate column.

Self-Awareness Check List

	Usually	Some-times	Seldom
I am aware of what I want when I talk with people.	_____	_____	_____
I communicate my intentions in words.	_____	_____	_____
I can distinguish between my intentions and my reactions to others.	_____	_____	_____
When what I want to do is not clear to me, I take the time to clarify my intentions.	_____	_____	_____
My intentions and my actions are congruent (I do what I say I will do).	_____	_____	_____

In considering my level of awareness and skill development relative to the material in this chapter, I think I (mention your strengths and weaknesses):

...and I thought I knew how to communicate!

CHAPTER 6

Speaking Personally

As previous chapters have pointed out, communication contains personal meaning. You would think, then, that persons interested in communicating the truths of their lives would communicate what is personally meaningful--I think. . . , I want. . . , I feel. . . etc. But often, entrenched habits speak for them in very different terms. Habit speaks of external facts, "You have a lovely place," instead of personal meanings, "I like what I see." Habit speaks in a loud, emphatic voice that asserts facts, "My boss is a tyrant. Do you know what she did to me yesterday?", instead of feelings, "I'm annoyed at her because. . . ." Habit speaks of objects, "Look at those dirty clothes on the floor. I've never seen a room as messy as this," instead of personal intentions, "I'd like for you to keep your room clean."

As the previous examples demonstrate, habit replaces personal meanings. Habit also prevents discovery of personal meanings. Suppose, for example, Gail is walking in the woods. She has the day off from work. The sun is shining and the day is warm and beautiful. If she were aware of her environment and her feelings, she would be enjoying what she sees and she would be feeling relaxed and happy. This particular day, that is not the case. Her habit has taken over, "My mother is a jerk. She bosses me around. It's kind of crazy, 'cause sometimes she's nice to us. I suppose I should love her and quit thinking bad thoughts about her, yet when it comes to visiting her I can't stand the thought of it. I couldn't believe what she did last week. . . ."

Habit can be strong, strong enough to actually prevent people from speaking their personal meanings, even when they really want to. Take a feeling of love, for example. Jim is in love, but listen to what he says, "She's really neat and I like her a lot, but I can't get myself to say, 'I love you,' to her; something else comes out." Take a need for self-expression: "I'm tired of having my feelings ignored, and I'd like to tell him that I want him to listen to me, but I don't say anything. I end up agreeing."

The purpose of this chapter is to help you develop your capability to speak your personal meanings clearly and directly. Consider how habit sabotages your efforts to do so.

Exposing Habit

What you learned much earlier in life stays with you and exerts its presence, regardless of whether or not it still has meaning for you. Have you heard adults say, "I don't like spinach?" I have. Just out of curiosity, I thought I'd pursue the matter with a friend who had expressed such an opinion. I was interested in whether his statement of dislike was an expression of current personal meaning or a worn-out habit carried over from earlier times. In my best translating manner, I said warmly, "So you don't like spinach." He said, "That's right. When I was a child my mother used to make me eat spinach. She cooked it until it got an awful green, and I've hated it ever since."

I asked, "About how old were you then?" He replied, "I don't know, but when I was maybe 8 or 9 she stopped making me eat it. I think she stopped serving it altogether about then."

"So it's been some 20 years since you've last eaten spinach," I commented. "Yes," he replied.

"As I look at it," I continued, "your habit of not liking spinach has prevented you from even trying it for all these years. I hear you telling me that you don't like spinach, as if you don't like it right now, when you haven't even tried it for 20 years. How do you know that if you tried spinach right now you wouldn't like it? You've changed in a great many ways in the last 20 years. Maybe spinach might be different for you now." Of course, he had no other answer than to reply lamely, "I don't like it," which is to say that every good habit defends its right to exist even when common sense suggests otherwise.

All of us have habits. Though the details and contents vary, there are some common themes. One is that habits that were useful in the past continue to present themselves as useful even when they no longer are. This false claim of usefulness assures old habits a place in the present. Consequently, these pretenders continue to produce negative consequences and block exploration of alternatives that could be useful now.

Another theme is that the habit extends itself into areas where it has no legitimate claim. What was true for our spinach hater was that he didn't like (at one time) the overly-cooked, dark green spinach his mother used to prepare. Through habit, what was once a specific distaste became generalized to "I don't like spinach, period." That includes lightly steamed spinach with hard boiled eggs, bacon or cheese; it includes spinach quiche and omelets; it includes a variety of spinach salads. His habit of disliking spinach prevented him from trying any form of spinach for 20 years.

A third theme is that habit operates below the level of conscious awareness. People think, feel and act without realizing that habit (not current personal meaning) is guiding them.

Finally, habit involves the whole organism. It takes over feelings, thoughts and actions in order to enforce and defend its presence. In particular, habit programs thoughts that perpetuate and defend its existence, for example, "I can't quit" or "That's just the way I am."

The following true stories illustrate these themes and help to expose the hold that habit can have on our lives.

Habit Inhibits Expression of Feeling

While she was attending college, Martha's mother wrote that her father had become sick, but it was nothing to worry about and he would be all right. Then, just before Thanksgiving, her mother called to say that her father had died. She hurried home, attended the funeral and was back in class three days later. She found it hard to concentrate on her studies. She became restless and had difficulty getting to sleep at night. She started to fall behind in her assignments and she didn't talk as much with her friends as she had previously. Those who knew her became concerned and tried to help in their own ways, but Martha said, "There's nothing to talk about. It's all over." She would bite her lip and turn away.

The truth was that she had a great deal to talk about. She had always loved her father. He had been good to her, even when they were at odds with each other. Losing him was a big blow; she was deeply sad. She was angry, too, because no one had told her how seriously ill her father had been, and because she hadn't had a chance to see him before he died. She felt she had disappointed him and wanted to tell him she was sorry, and to reassure him that everything was alright between them. She felt hurt and resentful that her mother had not told her what was going on but had told her sisters. Martha felt like she was being ignored and treated like a child.

Yes, she had a great deal to communicate, but habit prevented her. Her shoulders, neck and chin tensed up as her muscles physically choked back sobs and expressions of anger. Her shallow, controlled breathing served to prevent the release of feeling. Her aimless pacing back and forth, alternating with a slumping posture and vacant stare, were part of the package. These physical behaviors were reinforced by her habits of thinking. "Don't cry. That won't do any good. After all you are an adult and adults can control themselves; besides, you don't want to let people see you cry. That's a sign of weakness. Crying will do no good now; it won't bring him back to life. It's all over now so forget it. And how can you feel angry at your own mother for not telling you earlier? Shame! She's your mother and she was only acting with you in mind. You're an ungrateful girl to think bad thoughts about being neglected and hurt when your father is dead and your mother suffering. And remember, crying won't bring him back to life. It will only make your mother and your friends feel bad. You don't want to do that, do you?"

By preventing Martha from being aware of and expressing various aspects of her emotional state, habit exacted a terrible price in terms of mental health, personal relationships and success at college.

Habits Magnify Expression of Feeling

Habit can blow up an incident into an upset, can intensify feeling, spread it over a broader area and extend it through time. Making a mountain out of a molehill is the way some people describe this process.

John's teacher had some sharp words for him in class one day. She told him that he was not paying attention, that she didn't think he had studied very hard for the assignment and that he hadn't done a good job on his written work. She handed back his paper with a number of red marks indicating mistakes. John seethed, but didn't say anything as he brooded. As he left, he angrily pushed one of his classmates out of the way. When he got home, he yelled at his sister, took a kick at the cat and shut himself up in his room.

Although John was silent on the outside, his mind was racing furiously: "She has no right to treat me like that. Who does she think she is to deliberately embarrass me in front of my friends? I don't have to take that. She deliberately did that to me. She treated me unfairly and I've got a right to be bitter. Wait until I get my chance. I'll show her a thing or two about embarrassing people. She'll wish that she had never messed with me. Just because she has a college degree, she thinks she knows it all. We'll see about that."

John's habit, in maneuvering his thoughts in this way, succeeded in blowing a simple act of criticism out of all proportion. It prevented him from approaching the situation with thoughts that might counteract those of the habit. For example, John's habit prevented him from recalling times when his teacher had said some good words about his work. His habit prevented him from noticing that his teacher was annoyed at many people (not just him) that day. His habit prevented him from even considering the possibility that his teacher was more interested in his education than she was in embarrassing him. The sad part of all of this was the effect John's habit was having on his relationships, his other interests and his own satisfaction with life. Sooner or later he would blow up, and that would bring on additional problems.

Habits Substitute Themselves for Wants

Just as feelings can be covered up, inhibited, disguised or distorted by habit, so can want.

Sue wanted to say "No." She was tired of being a doormat. When other people asked her to do something, she might at first say, "No," but not in a firm voice. When they persisted, she would end up saying "Yes" and dislike herself for being such a pushover. Her thoughts would whisper, "Other people are important. You don't want to make them unhappy, do you? People should be nice to each other and so you should be nice to others. If it's important to others for you to do something, if it will help them, then do it. You don't want to lose friends; you don't want to create friction so go along with them, and maybe they'll like you better."

The price she paid for not asserting her own wants was a loss of self-esteem. She wanted to respect herself, to know that she could stand up to others when necessary. She wanted to say "No," but her people-pleasing habit intruded. Her want didn't get satisfied; instead she often felt depressed, angry at herself and still wanting that elusive self-respect.

"Should" Habits Block Wants

During high school, Jake had taken the courses that were required for admission to college. He was moving in that direction, but really didn't know why. He felt a vague uneasiness about going to a university; he found it difficult to make specific plans or to think about what course of study he might pursue. He basically avoided active consideration of the whole topic and he wasn't very enthusiastic when he was forced to talk about it. When he asked himself why he was going to college, he heard an authoritative voice in his head saying, "Of course you're going to college. That's the only way to obtain the education you need to get a good job and get ahead in the world. People in your social class go to college. Your parents and their friends are all college educated. They'd be ashamed of you if you weren't. You wouldn't fit in and you probably wouldn't meet the kind of people that you need to know if you really want to get ahead in the world. You just think you don't want to go to college. You'll go and you'll find that it's really fun and you'll enjoy it and later you'll be pleased that you did." Messages like this presented themselves in Jake's head every time he seriously tried to question whether or not he really wanted to go to college.

Communicating Personal Meanings

Habits, in a variety of forms, carry over from the past to bias, interfere with or inhibit our present lives. We need to become aware of such habits so we can take steps to put them aside. When we experience what is really happening within us, we can choose to act on and communicate our own personal meanings. The following diagram adapted from Couple Communication (see Postscript) illustrates some of the possibilities.

Dimensions of Personal Meanings

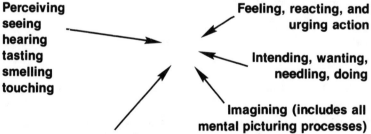

Perceiving
seeing
hearing
tasting
smelling
touching

Feeling, reacting, and
urging action

Intending, wanting,
needling, doing

Imagining (includes all
mental picturing processes)

Thinking, (and all other verbal
thinking processes) for example, remembering,
anticipating, generalizing, deciding, assuming,
interpreting, integrating, reasoning

Most people would not (and probably could not) communicate all of their personal meanings at one time. If someone wanted to, a simple situation might be communicated like this: "I **see** the cake in the oven; I **remember** that I put in all of the ingredients; I **imagine** that my children will like it; I intend to take it from the oven when it's done; I **feel** happy about having it ready for their party." As personal meanings are in a constant state of flux, this person's communication would necessarily change even as it was being communicated: "Now I **hear** the doorbell; I **wonder** who's there; I'm a **little nervous** about leaving the cake, etc."

To Communicate or Not To Communicate Personal Meanings

Suppose that you have developed your self-awareness so that you're in a position to either choose an old process, such as instinct or habit, or to express current personal meanings. When might you want to stay with the old?

One situation would be in routine social interactions. A friend approaches and asks, "Hi, how are you?" A frank reply of feeling is not expected nor even welcome (usually). Your habit, "Fine, thank you," is considered an appropriate response.

Other situations in which actual meanings are seldom communicated include those instances 1) when other people are trying to take advantage of you, and 2) when you just want to play (as with the waitress and the pie-eating customer of the preceding chapter).

We have to remember that other people expect us to communicate in traditional ways. Often, we have to play the traditional game so as not to alienate those with whom we deal. Thus, we may sometimes be aware of our personal meanings but choose to go with our habits and communicate in traditional language. We can then switch to personal meanings the moment misunderstanding, confusion or conflict seem eminent.

Being aware of personal meanings is more difficult to do than it is to write about. Practicing the exercises that follow can get you moving in the direction of increased awareness.

Skill Builders

Chapter 6: SPEAKING PERSONALLY

6.1 Habitual Reactions

Purpose:
To help you identify reactions that are often not accessible to your awareness.

Directions:
Have you ever had a doctor tap you sharply just below your knee cap so that your leg moved (without you moving it)? If so, you know what a reflex is like. With that knowledge you also understand what habitual responses are usually like--automatic, nonthinking reactions to particular verbal and nonverbal messages. Because such reactions are immediate and automatic, you don't have a chance to consider responses that might be more appropriate.

In dangerous situations, automatic responses may serve you well, but in daily life they often prevent you from hearing what is really being said and interfere with your ability to respond appropriately and in your best interests.

List words, pictures, vocal sounds or physical actions that seem to trigger automatic responses on your part.

Triggers (as you see them):

_____

_____

_____

To find out more about your automatic reactions, ask people who know you well to tell you what words, pictures, vocal sounds or physical actions you react to.

Triggers (as others see them):

_____

_____

_____

Write down responses you could make and actions that would serve as alternatives to your habitual reactions.

Alternative responses:

_____

_____

_____

Suggestion: Get a friend to help you try out these various alternatives. Choose an alternative response you want to make. Ask your friend to do or speak the particular trigger so you can practice responding in the new way. Repeat this process several times so your new response becomes more natural.

To make this exercise a little more realistic, ask your friend to introduce the trigger, without warning, while you are in the midst of conversation about an unrelated topic. Repeat this process several times and incorporate other triggers and other responses that you would like to try out.

6.2 Becoming Aware of Perceptions

Purpose:
To sharpen your awareness of how your perceiving takes place.

Directions:
Look around you. What do you see. . . . Take your mind off of what you have been doing and allow yourself to see what there is to see. . . . Notice details of color, size, shape and texture. . . . Allow yourself to see what is really there. Now let your eyes move to see what else there is. . . . Keep your awareness on what you see. . . . If you find yourself thinking about something, let the thoughts go and pay attention to what you see. (long pause)

Now notice what you hear. . . . Allow yourself to hear sounds that you weren't aware of before. . . . Silently say the words, "I hear. . ." and complete the sentence with whatever sound is in your awareness. Repeat this process several times. (long pause)

Now move your awareness back to what you see. . . . Silently speak the words, "I see. . ." and complete the sentence with whatever is in your awareness at the time. Repeat this process several times. (long pause)

Now consider this. Sometimes you intentionally look at something. Other times your natural habits of seeing, unaided by any conscious effort direct your vision. Explore your natural habits of seeing. . . . Allow yourself to see without trying to see anything in particular. . . . Don't intentionally move your eyes, but allow them to move in whatever way your natural habits direct. . . . What do your eyes tend to focus on? shapes? colors? textures? patterns. . . ? Do your eyes tend to move slowly or rapidly. . . ? Do they stay in one place or move around?

Now take charge of your seeing and intentionally look at something. . . , then intentionally look at something else. . . . What can you observe about the differences between your natural habits and your intentional ways of seeing the world? (long pause)

Move your eyes to look again at something you've looked at before. . . . Discover some new aspect of what you have seen previously. . . .

Each moment of seeing is a different experience. . . . You never see anything in exactly the same way twice. . . . You never see all of anything. . . . Now look around you. . . . Notice that even though you have been seeing, there are still aspects of your visible world that you hadn't noticed before. (long pause)

Realizing that you can't see all of what is there, realizing that what you see varies from time to time, perhaps you'll be less likely to make authoritative statements about what is actually there. (Take a moment to reflect or experiment further with your awareness of the ways in which you perceive the world.)

6.3 Perceiving and Interpreting

Purpose:
To sharpen your awareness of the distinction between perception and interpretation.

Directions:
Following each number below is a pair of responses, one indicating perception, the other indicating interpretation. For each pair, check the one that indicates perception.

1. A. He didn't speak to me today.
   B. He's unfriendly.

2. A. She said she would be here by noon. She arrived at 12:30.
   B. She was late.

3. A. He looks both ways before crossing the street.
   B. He is careful.

4. A. He watches television every afternoon.
   B. He's lazy.

5. A. Those kids are playing dangerously.
   B. Those kids are kicking a ball in the street.

6. A. He retired about ten years ago.
   B. He's an old man.

7. A. He is pacing back and forth.
   B. He's anxious.

8. A. He doesn't send me flowers or buy me any presents.
   B. He doesn't love me.

6.4 Awareness of Physical Sensations of Feeling

Purpose:
To help you identify the physical sensations that form the basis for your feelings.

Directions:
Insert one of the following words--anxious, irritated, upset, frustrated, angry, sad--in the first blank, and complete the sentence with whatever is true. Complete all three sentences in this manner.

I get _____ when _____

I get _____ when _____

I get _____ when _____

From the three sentences above, pick one of the feeling words that follow "get." Think of a time when you experienced that feeling. Let your imagination recreate that scene and make it real for you right now. When you start to experience the feeling, answer the following questions:

What are you aware of inside your body?

Where are your sensations of feeling located?

Focus on those sensations and describe them in as much detail, as you can.

What changes do you notice in your hands? your face? your legs? your throat and breathing?

What is your body urging you to do?

How do you communicate any or all of this?

If your feeling had words, it would say. . . .

...and I thought I knew how to communicate!

6.5 Awareness of a Source of Intentions

Purpose:

Directions that serve to focus your awareness on your intentions and on how you express them.

Directions:

1. Think about a close friend. If that close friend were to walk up to you right now, what would you say and do? What would be your intention in saying (doing) that? Where does that intention come from? (Of course one answer is that the intention comes from you, but can you be more specific?)

   How does your energy get focused to bring that intention to life? How much of your intention message is conveyed in your words and how much by the sound of your voice or by your physical movement? What other intentions do you have toward that friend? How do you express them? How might you express those intentions more directly in words? To reinforce that verbal message, what would you be doing? How would your voice sound?

2. How do you usually indicate to people that you would like to get to know them better? Could you convey your intentions more directly through words and appropriate physical movements that leave little room for doubt as to what you intend? What do you imagine would happen if you were to do that? What keeps you from it?

3. There are many times you have multiple intentions. For example, suppose you want to be by yourself because you're feeling tired and tense and a good friend approaches and wants to talk with you about a matter in which you have little interest. Nonetheless, you want to maintain your friendship. What would you say and do? What do you imagine your message conveys? How could you convey both of your intentions more clearly (wanting to be by yourself and wanting to maintain your friendship?)

6.6 Separating Intentions, Feelings and Habits of Thinking

Purpose:

To bring personal situations into your awareness in such a way that intention, feeling and thought habits can be distinguished.

Directions:

The purpose of this exercise is to help you move through confusion or doubt by helping you to identify the various urges that pull/push you in different directions.

To review: *intention arises from within; energy is generated and focused on action that can attain a needed/wanted goal.* That energy is experienced as an urge. *Feeling responses are provoked from without.* A person or thing triggers a feeling response which includes an urge to move (in fear, away from; in love, toward, etc.) Reactive thoughts (often experienced as internal voices) are produced in the mind. They urge that some particular action should or shouldn't be taken. Following is an example of how the three interact.

Tom wants food to satisfy his hunger. He goes to a grocery store and moves down the aisle (intention) with that purpose in mind. On the way he spots his girl friend in the next aisle. He is attracted to her and starts to move rapidly toward her (feeling/urge). A voice in his head (habit) says, "Don't rush; play it cool. Don't show her how eager you are to see her."

1. Recall a time when you felt confused, torn or undecided. What were your wants/intentions? What were you feeling. . . ? Identify the person or object that seemed to be the cause of that feeling. . . . What did your feeling urge you to do. . . ? What did your inner voices or thoughts tell you to do or not to do?

2. Get an image in mind of a current relationship that is important to you. . . . Become aware of what you intend/want in that relationship. . . ? Become aware of feeling urges that come about as a response to the other person. . . . Become aware of any internal voices that are telling you what you should or shouldn't do. . . . Assuming that your intention indicates the fundamental direction you want your relationship to take, make a plan to follow through on it.

...and I thought I knew how to communicate!

CHAPTER 7

Building Quality Relationships

"Our marriage is on the rocks. I just can't get through to my husband. He won't listen, and he doesn't understand that I feel we have a problem. Our daughter, Wendy, has grown silent and less cooperative around the house. I think something has happened at school but she doesn't seem to want to talk about it. Last night I mentioned to him that I was concerned about Wendy. He shrugged it off again, saying there was no reason to be concerned. He said I get upset over nothing and he walked out to go watch TV. I felt like what I said or wanted didn't matter. I felt rejected and alone, and I was reminded that many of our conversations end like this. He wouldn't have to do anything differently if only he would listen to me. When people don't listen to me, I know that they think that I'm not worth listening to."

In the paragraph above, Marlys is talking about her relationship with her husband. She had one of those golden insights into relationships: "When people don't listen to me, I know that they think I'm not worth listening to." "Know" is probably too strong a word, but let's not let that get in the way of acknowledging the truth of her statement. Marlys and the rest of us form judgments of other people based on how they act towards us. When our communications are shunted aside and belittled, when our opinions are not respected, we start to question ourselves and our listeners' intentions towards us.

We Seek Understanding From Others

We want others to allow us to speak our minds, to listen without doubting, interrupting, changing the subject or putting us down. When that happens we feel understood. We gain a sense of self-worth. We believe that others are interested in us and care about us.

Allowing Yourself to Understand Others

Can you allow yourself to listen? You don't have to agree with everything others say, but before you disagree, can you give their opinions the hearing and respect that you would like yours to be given? You don't have to believe that everything they say is factually true, but before you cast doubts, can you grant them the opportunity to speak? You may have something of importance to say, but by cutting other people off to speak for yourself, you indicate to them that they are not as important as you are. By simply listening, you can do a great deal, probably more than you now think, to preserve and build personal and social relationships.

Listening for Meanings

Recall that in Chapter 3, personal meanings were described as consisting of feelings, wants, reactions, thoughts, beliefs and so on. When you want to effectively relate to other people, *listen for their personal meanings with a goal of sharing your understanding (translation) of those meanings.* That can be a tremendously rewarding process because meanings are the very content of life. Listen to meanings speak:

"I am my **reaction** to skiing, my liking for apple pie, my **thoughts** about nuclear war, my **concerns** for unemployed persons, my fantasies about the future, my **memories** of growing up as a child, my **ideas** about what makes people happy, my **interests** in seeing new places, my **caring** for my children, my **desire** to take care of myself by jogging, my **thoughts** about helping others build better relationships, my **plans** for the summer, my **interest** in jazz, my **pride** in my work, my **satisfaction** at having a job I like, my sadness when a good friend dies. Much that is important about my life and my sense for life is embodied in my meanings. If you listen to my meanings, I will feel understood and accepted. I will value myself more because you have listened."

Translating and Communicating Meanings

Personal meanings are easy to understand when a speaker communicates them in a self-revealing way, as I did in the preceding chapter. A problem arises when meanings are not openly revealed, when people speak of other people, events, or things without revealing their own meanings. "Pat, that's a neat sweater. Where did you get it?" asks Bonnie (with no mention of her personal meanings).

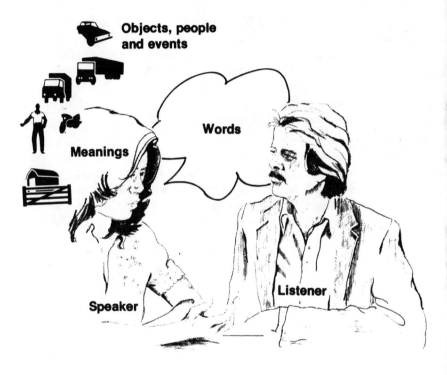

The diagram reminds us that Bonnie's words are necessarily an expression of her personal meanings. Taking a meaning-making perspective, Pat translates her words as having a meaning of liking, "She likes my sweater." With that in mind, Pat responds to Bonnie, "Glad you like it," or "Do you like it?" (depending on how confident he is of his understanding of her meaning). In either case, his reply focuses on Bonnie's meaning and opens the door to a more personal way of relating.

If he is not tuned in to her meaning, he will likely notice her references to facts, "sweater" and "Where did you get it?" He answers her factual question. In that case, the conversation has moved away from the personal and Pat has lost a golden opportunity to strengthen their relationship.

When speakers make factual statements, there are times when translations seem obvious, redundant or beside the point. For example, suppose a speaker were to ask, "What time is it?" A translated reply, "You're concerned that you may be late," seems foolish (even if true). Especially when statements are brief, for example, "She lives in Chicago," it may be best to simply acknowledge the communication and to encourage the speaker to continue. Nodding your head, leaning forward or saying "I'm listening," or "Go on," usually accomplish this. Another possibility is to translate vocal sounds if feeling or intention seem to be important.

Translating and acknowledging/encouraging show that you're interested in your speaker and that you understand and accept the speaker's viewpoint. By inviting further sharing on the speaker's part, you show respect or liking. Another positive aspect of translating/encouraging is that while you're translating/encouraging, you're not talking in ways that create distance between you and the others. You are not finding fault, blaming, interrupting, changing the subject, becoming defensive, arguing, giving unwanted advice, jumping to conclusions, being cute, being sarcastic or withdrawing. Keep this in mind as you read the following dialogue in which a father relates to his son by serving as a listener/translator/encourager.

Son: Things haven't been going very well at work.

Father: You seem kind of discouraged about that.

Son: I sure am. My boss thinks that another employee is doing much better than I am. This other guy gets all the breaks, the best assignments and all that, and I have to take what's left over.

Father: (nods in understanding) It sounds to me like you're just a little bit angry at your boss and jealous of this other guy.

Son: I'm not really jealous, I mean, I don't blame Jack for taking what he can get. It's my boss that gets to me. He's just not giving me a chance.

Father: Go ahead. I'm listening.

Son: Well today I showed him this plan I had worked up. I spent several hours after work last night getting it ready. All the boss said was, "Put it on my desk, I'll look at it later."

Father: Uh-huh, and that disappointed you.

Son: It sure did. Here I expected to get some recognition and all I got was the brush off.

Father: So yesterday, you really tried to show him that you could do a good job, and he wouldn't even take the time to acknowledge you.

Son: That's right, and it's like that all the time. This isn't the first time he's passed me by. I'm fed up. With him there I don't have a chance to go anywhere. If I told him how I felt, it would get even worse.

Father: I get it that you're pretty discouraged and haven't yet found a way of making things better.

Speaking Personal Meanings

Listening is one way of building relationships; speaking one's personal meanings is another. I mean more than talking about topics such as school, job, vacations, food or the weather. All of us know how to do that, but that type of communication only goes so far. I mean sharing what's really going on with you—what you like and don't like, how you feel about the other person, what you want in life, what concerns you have and so on. Sometimes, this means expressing a reaction that seems negative to the other person such as, "I feel neglected when you're late," or "I get angry at you when you leave that sloppy mess on the floor." Sometimes, it means expressing positive aspects of your relationship, for example, "I appreciate it when you get the dishes done promptly like that," or "I like it when you rub my back." Sharing personal meanings, even the seemingly negative ones, can lead to a deeper relationship. That's the idea underlying the Johari Window (see J. Luft's book, Of Human Interaction, Palo Alto, CA, National Press, 1969).

Person 1		Person 2	
Blind	**Open**	**Open**	**Blind**
Unknown	**Hidden**	**Hidden**	**Unknown**

The Open quadrants signify information that is known to both persons. The Hidden quadrant of Person 1 signifies information that is known to Person 1, but not to Person 2. The Hidden quadrant of Person 2 signifies information known to Person 2 but not to Person 1.

The Blind quadrant of Person 1 signifies information about Person 1, not known to Person 1 but known to Person 2. For example, Person 1 doesn't know that calling Person 2 late at night annoys Person 2. The reverse relationship holds true for the Blind quadrant of Person 2. The Unknown quadrants signify information, perhaps locked in the subconscious of each person, that is not readily available to either.

When two people first meet, their respective Open quadrants are quite small since they have not yet had the opportunity to reveal much about themselves. As they talk, the Open quadrants get larger, how much larger depends on how willing they are to share with each other.

Self-Disclosure

Person 1

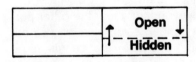

Open quadrants get larger as information that was previously "hidden" is self-disclosed. (As the Hidden quadrant gets smaller, the Open one gets larger.) An example of self-disclosure is: "I haven't told you this before, but I've been seeing Sally."

...and I thought I knew how to communicate!

Feedback: Giving and Receiving

Open quadrants get larger as information that was previously "blind" (unknown) becomes known. (As the Blind quadrant gets smaller, the Open one gets larger.) For example, Person 1 was "blind" to the fact that Person 2 became annoyed at night when Person 1 called. When Person 2 tells Person 1 of being annoyed at the calls, Person 1 is no longer "blind" to it.

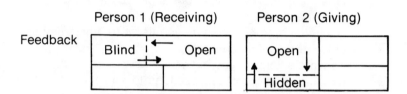

Notice that, in feedback, the speaker's Open quadrant gets larger as that speaker gives (self-discloses) feedback and that the the listener's Open quadrant gets larger as the listener receives the feedback.

Where Do You Stand?

In everyday life, most relationships reach an impasse sooner or later. That happens, in part, because one or both parties have been unwilling to self-disclose what's been hidden or to listen to and accept feedback from the other.

Questions:
1. How much are you willing to open up and share your hidden meanings? What information about yourself and your reactions to others do you withhold?
2. How often and how well do you listen to others self-disclose personal meanings?
3. To what extent do you indicate that you are receptive to hearing other people's reactions to you (both positive and negative)? (When you convey your willingness to listen, others usually feel less afraid to share.)
4. To what extent do you share your reactions to others (positive and negative) when those others seem receptive? (Providing unwanted feedback is usually not welcome.)

As you think about different people, you'll find that your answers vary from person to person. If you have any caring relationships that seem stuck, you can use your answers to gain insight into what you might do to get those relationships moving again.

Dimensions of Personal Meaning

Personal meanings are multidimensional. They involve interpreting, imagining, feeling, wanting and perceiving. People generally have a habit of omitting one or more of these in their interactions with others. For example, a woman I know tells me that her husband talks about business, money, the children, politics and his various interests, but almost never reveals his feelings. She sometimes asks him directly how he feels. She says that his replies, often a shoulder shrug or "I'm not sure," seem evasive to her. She assumes that he really does have feelings but for some reason is unable to express them. For her, that gets in the way of their relationship.

...and I thought I knew how to communicate!

Maintaining a healthy relationship requires a willingness to disclose in various dimensions that pertain to issues like spending money, visiting relatives, cleaning house or seeing friends. Each person in the relationship has thoughts, beliefs and expectations about such issues; each has feelings toward the other and toward various solutions and ideas the other might propose. Each has wants. If the husband, for example, only says that he doesn't like his wife's ideas, and omits stating his own wants, a key dimension is missing; frustration often results. If his wife fails to give her reactions to his expression of feelings, again a piece is missing. For neither to mention what they have seen and heard (as opposed to what they think they know) leaves out the the dimension of perception, the aspect of meaning that lies closest to whatever facts there are.

In your relationship, if you struggle with on-going issues, self-disclose various dimensions of your meanings; draw out your partner's reactions to these; ask for important dimensions that seem to be missing. Such discussions require time, energy and commitment, but they can be counted on to achieve constructive resolutions of the issues and to build a better relationship.

Meanings Don't Always Come Easily

A number of suggestions have been made as to how relationships might be improved. If you find it difficult to follow through with these, try to identify the habits and feelings that hold you back (fear of being rejected, for example). Look at your willingness to put aside the barriers so that others can enter your world. Look at your willingness to accept other people with whatever frailties they have. If you have reservations about another person, if in your heart you believe the other is somehow deficient and in need of change, if you maintain a protective shell, then you probably have erected barriers that will make it difficult for you to relate to the other on a meaningful level.

If you have trouble listening/encouraging/translating or if you have trouble self-disclosing your personal meanings, look deep inside to see what your intentions toward the other person really are. You may find that you don't really have a strong desire to be any closer to this person. (Perhaps you just thought you should have a relationship for security, adventure, appearance or convenience.) If, however, you become aware of a clear intention to move toward the other person and follow through in the suggested ways but don't get the results you want, try to create an accepting climate so that any fears the other may have are eased. Consider stating your intentions directly: "I want to work this out with you," "I want to get closer to you," or whatever your intentions might be. If you still don't get results, check out the other's intentions toward you. If the other doesn't want to move in the same direction you do, trying harder may only add to your frustration. Sometimes, two people just aren't meant for each other.

Nonverbal Relationship Messages

Physical movements and voices convey messages—feelings, intentions, reactions and interpretations—just as words do. Nonverbal messages either reinforce verbal ones, make them seem ambiguous, or contradict them. A nonverbal message may be the only message when verbal communication is absent. John is watching TV, not talking to his wife, Jayne. His silence conveys a message. It may not be an intended message, but Jayne, having eyes and ears, interprets what she sees and hears. Jayne wonders if he's troubled or angry. In either case, she'd like to talk with him about it or to help in some way. From Jayne's perspective, John's silent TV watching is a barrier to their relating well. (There may or may not be a barrier of some kind for John, too.) For this situation to get unstuck, one of them needs to do or say something. For example, he might give her a kiss or some other friendly message before he sits down, or he might say, "I'm tense, but it's nothing to do with you; watching TV will help me relax." She might say, "I'm feeling left out, I'd like a little time with you this evening."

People see how other people act; they hear how others' voices sound. What they see and hear they interpret, react to, feel and think about. For some people, what they see and hear speaks louder than words. To have satisfactory relationships, people must pay attention to their own nonverbals and to how they interpret the nonverbals of others. Often they need to check out their interpretations. One way to do this is by giving feedback, for example, "When I see you watching TV and you don't speak to me, I wonder if there is a problem between us."

Summary

There are many different ideas as to what makes a quality relationship. One idea is that of being "open" (mutual sharing): its opposite is being "closed" (silence, secrets and manipulation). Most relationships lie somewhere between the two extremes. If the idea of a more open relationship appeals to you, then you may want to take steps to move in that direction. Acknowledging/accepting/translating, self-disclosing, and giving and receiving feedback may be just what you need.

I'm not suggesting that these are the only ways to build quality relationships. I'm not suggesting that techniques can provide a quick fix to a troubled relationship or magically move any particular one from 0 to 10. Quality relationships usually take time to build and the journey is more likely to be made a step at a time than in one giant leap.

If your intentions are to develop a deeper relationship or move one beyond a stuck place, then consider listening/acknowledging/translating, self-disclosing and giving and receiving feedback. I hope they work for you!

Skill Builders

7.1 Public and Private Aspects of Self

Purpose:
To help you increase your awareness of what you do and do not reveal to others, and to assess the possible benefits of being more disclosing.

Directions:
Out of available materials, construct a "self" (use a box, crayons, bag, envelope, etc.) On the outside, put information (words, pictures or drawings) that represents what you usually reveal to others about yourself. On the inside, put information that you less frequently reveal (usually keep hidden). On a separate piece of paper, write down a secret about yourself that you rarely (if ever) reveal to anyone. Fold and seal this secret and hide it away in the "self" you constructed. Don't be in a hurry to develop your "self." Take time to become aware of what you disclose and what you hide.

If you're doing this exercise by yourself, imagine that you are meeting someone for the second or third time and that you like that person. Imagine that you are sharing the public part of yourself. What are your thoughts about revealing something that you have hidden? What prevents you from sharing that? What might you gain if you did? What could you do that would make it easier for the other person to self-disclose what was hidden? If that person did reveal something that is usually kept hidden, what response would be good on your part (assuming you want to develop your relationship further)?

If you're doing this exercise with another person who has also built a "self," share whatever you wish to do of your "self" with the other. Later, discuss your sharing experience, using the questions in the preceding paragraph as a guide.

7.2 Giving Constructive Feedback

Purpose:
To practice giving feedback in constructive ways.

Directions:
Many persons avoid giving negative feedback because they are afraid it will hurt or "put down" the other person or trigger conflict and rejection. Certainly that can happen when feedback takes the traditional form of blaming, accusing or fault-finding. Feedback is less likely to have effects like that when it is communicated as personal meaning (I see. . . , I feel. . . , and so forth). Examples of both traditional and meaning-making feedback are presented in the following situations.

Situation:
Your friend has a habit of borrowing your things and not bringing them back (and you don't like that).

Traditional Responses

Accusing: You're always borrowing things and never bringing them back. You're inconsiderate:

Lying: It's all right. I didn't really need them anyway.

Personal-Meaning Response (Feedback): I'm aware that you've borrowed several of my things (it would help to be specific). I'm getting annoyed, because it's been a long time and I don't have any of them back. I want to keep our friendship and I also want my things back.

Situation: Person I has started calling Person 2 late at night to talk about interesting, but nonessential matters. Person 2 gets irritated by this as the calling continues.

Traditional Responses

Blaming: You bother me at night. You don't think about me; you rattle on and on about things that don't really matter. You make me mad and then I can't sleep.

Lying: If you want to call me, it's OK. I can always sleep on Sunday.

...and I thought I knew how to communicate!

Personal-Meaning Response (Feedback): I need some time for myself at night and I need my sleep. Your calls at night are getting to me. I'd appreciate it if you would call earlier. I do want to keep you as a friend but I can't go on pretending that it's all right.

Think of a specific situation (involving another person) in which you get a negative feeling toward that person. Describe the situation. Then write down a personal-meaning feedback response (which includes what you perceive, how you feel, what you want and perhaps what you think).

Your situation: _____

_____

_____

Your personal-meaning feedback response: _____

_____

_____

When and where might you consider giving feedback to that person? If your answer is "Never," what are you afraid might happen?

Identify other negative situations. Create personal meaning, feedback responses and consider when and where you might actually communicate them.

7.3 Food for Thought

Purpose:
To identify possible risks and benefits of self-disclosing and giving feedback.

Directions:
Please respond to the following questions.

1. What are the risks in being self-disclosing? When is it better not to be open? Give examples.
2. Can a person self-disclose nonverbally or behaviorally? Give examples.
3. What are some possible benefits of self-disclosing?
4. What are the risks in giving feedback? Give examples.
5. How can one person encourage others to self-disclose or give feedback?
6. How can people minimize the risks involved in self-disclosing and in giving and receiving feedback?

It may be helpful for you to voice your understanding of the other's perception of the situation. For example, you could say, "From your position, I can see how you got upset," or "If I were in your shoes, I guess I might be mad too."

7.4 Awareness of the Immediacy of Personal Meanings

Purpose:
To focus on your immediate experience of various aspects of your meaning-making process.

Direcetions:
Find another person who can participate with you in this exercise. Sit side by side silently looking at what is in front of you.

Try to look without thinking, without words coming into your mind . . . . Observe in a pure nonverbal way—noticing color as color. . . texture as texture. . . shape as shape. . . relationship as relationship. . . (long pause).

As you are observing, notice the words that enter your awareness; these mark the beginning of your interpretations of what you see.

Let your gaze move around, stopping now and then to observe what there is before you. As you observe, can you become aware of the distinction between observing and interpreting ? (long pause)

As you move your gaze, stopping now and then to observe, can you become aware of the flow from observation to interpretation? (long pause)

Now notice that sometimes, when you focus your observations, you can become aware of subtle changes in your own feelings. . . and in sensations such as breathing. . . tension. . . facial expressions . . warmth. . . . Looking at your own body or looking at your partner may make some of these changes more noticeable. Try looking at your partner. . . . When you notice changing sensations in your body you are experiencing the reactive, feeling part of your meaning-making process. You are discovering how feelings sometimes creep into meaning as a natural part of the observation process.

While looking at your partner, become aware of changes in your observations or interpretations as your feelings change. . .

Switch your gaze from your partner to some object, so that you can no longer see your partner. As you focus on this object, are you in any way still affected by the experience of having looked at your partner? Did that experience of looking at your partner affect what you see now?

Continue looking at an object. (Do not look at your partner.) Pure observation is what you are after . . . (long pause). Shift your gaze to another object. Notice words that come into your mind and sensations that arise. . . . Continue to be aware of how words and sensations attach themselves to observations. . . . Continue to become aware of any carry-over as you move from one set of observations to another. . . .

Turn to look at your partner again. Look at your partner's face for a couple of minutes and try to really see this other person . . . I want you to look at your partner and simply be aware of facial details. . . . Become aware of the characteristics of your partner's features—colors. . . , shapes. . . and textures. . . . , how the face moves or doesn't move. . . . . I want you to become deeply aware of, to really see this other person. . . . Is there anything going on in you now that makes it difficult for you to focus your attention on your partner? If something else is competing for your attention, take a little time to become more aware of this. . . . Become aware of how your sensations, images and thoughts limit your ability to see all that is there. . . .

Now look at your partner. . . . Speak to each other. Share your experience of the last five minutes. Begin with "I."

7.5 Barriers to Interaction

Purpose:
Through imagery, to help you identify various habit barriers that prevent you from developing closer personal relationships.

Direcetions:
In the previous exercise it was suggested that your mental processes affect what you actually see and feel. In that exercise you may have discovered that your mind was so influential that you found it hard to look at your partner's face for any length of time. Your vision, under the control of a habit which urged you not to stare or be rude, may have turned away.

Emotions can limit your vision; thought habits can limit your vision; previously formed judgments and beliefs can limit your vision. Generally, your tendency is to see that which supports your feelings and beliefs. You may fail to see that which would call these feelings and beliefs into question.

Allow yourself to recall a recent interaction with someone you care about. What were you thinking at the time? How did that affect your ability to see and hear all that was happening? If you had been less under the influences of your thoughts, what might you have seen that you actually missed? How might you have interpreted your interaction differently?

Repeat this exercise, recalling different people and different circumstances, especially interactions which didn't flow like you wanted them to flow. What can you discover about how your attitudes, beliefs, thoughts and expectations restrict your ability to see and interpret what is there?

7.6 Building Relationships

Purpose:
To identify ways of developing quality relationships other than by self-disclosing, giving feedback and listening/translating.

Direcetions:
Self-disclosing, giving and receiving feedback, listening for and translating personal meanings are ways to build and maintain relationships. What are some other ways? Try to be as specific as you can. Make a list. Show it to other people. See if they agree. If they have other ideas, add them to your list. Keep your list handy for future reference.

Ways to Build and Maintain Relationships

1. _____

2. _____

3. _____

4. _____

5. _____

6. _____

7. _____

8. _____

9. _____

10. _____

...and I thought I knew how to communicate!

CHAPTER 8

Constructive Ways of Dealing With Criticism and Conflict

I'm speaking to those of you who have a history of emotionally reacting to criticism, blame, sarcasm, accusation, fault-finding or conflict. Your history probably extends all the way back to childhood. My three year old came home last week crying her eyes out because a playmate had called her "Garbagehead."

Upon hearing names you thought were not true, some of you may have cried and sought help as my daughter did; some may have become defensive, "I'm not a garbagehead." Others may have counterattacked, "You're a garbagehead and a rotten potato too"; and still others may have quietly harbored resentment against the name-caller. All of these responses have one characteristic in common—an emotional reaction triggered by a particular communication (sometimes merely a word) somebody thought was wrong.

Some emotional reactions are valuable; others bring trouble. Either way, as you grow older you carry your emotional-reaction habit with you. Your thoughts try to justify your habit: "I can't help it, that's the way I am; and besides I have a right to get upset when someone says things about me that aren't true."

For better or for worse, you're partly governed by habits that developed naturally as you learned traditional ways of speaking and reacting. These habits are so much a part of you that it may be difficult to conceive of other ways of responding. In this chapter, I want to open the door to some other ways. Can you be open to looking at some other possibilities, even though they might, at the moment, seem strange, impractical and far-out?

Criticism is Growth Producing

Criticism, blame, accusation, sarcasm and other forms of verbal attack tend to put us on the defensive. We may counterattack, defend ourselves, leave the scene or simply pretend to listen (letting any offensive phrases go in one ear and out the other). These reactions are often self-defeating, as when a student reacts to a teacher, "I'm not going to listen to you tell me how to improve my spelling."

People learn skills such as spelling by accepting the criticisms of those who know more, then learning what is considered correct. The same idea holds true for skills involved in playing musical instruments, reading, solving problems and building relationships.

It is often difficult to listen to criticism and other negative statements because the speaker may exaggerate and communicate superiority, anger and rejection. Thus, the remarks seem unfair. Martha says to her friend, Sally, "You blabbermouth. You talk when you shouldn't; you talk too much and you don't keep secrets."

Yet whether or not it seems fair, people have little to gain by rejecting criticism outright before they can examine it to see if any valuable information is contained therein. Unfair attacks can be of as much value as fair ones. If Sally can listen to Martha and find out the perceived basis for the attack, Sally may learn something that can help her to better relate to Martha and to others in the future.

To get ahead in the world, you need people to call attention to what's wrong so you can identify what blocks your growth and your relationships. You need that information even though you may not like it. The point is that you need it; the more you get, the more you can learn (up to a point). Thus, you should welcome criticism, seek it out and even thank those who risk their relationships with you in telling you what you won't want to hear. I know that sounds like strange advice, but bear with me and consider some possibilities.

...and I thought I knew how to communicate!

Strategies for Dealing with Criticism and Conflict

Translating Thoughts

Words, posing as statements of fact about you ("You're a blab-bermouth"), express the personal meanings of the speaker. Therefore, such statements can be translated as meanings. Suppose someone accuses you, "You didn't do that right!" You can translate and reply, "You apparently don't like what I did," or "You have some thoughts about what I should do." Translating critical remarks is an alternative to becoming defensive, counterattacking, covering up or withdrawing.

Translating Feelings

In Chapter 4, it was suggested that vocal sounds and physical activity can be translated into feeling terms. That suggestion also applies to criticism, blaming and sarcasm. Suppose someone accuses you, "You didn't do that right!" and in that person's voice you hear the loudness and intensity that you associate with anger. You could translate, "You seem angry with me," or "Apparently, you're upset with me," then wait for a clearer picture to emerge of what upset the speaker. Translation of feeling is an alternative to becoming defensive, counterattacking, covering up or withdrawing.

Acknowledging Possible Truth

In Chapter 2, it was suggested that words don't tell the total truth about events in the world, nor do they tell total lies (usually). When hearing criticism, a possible reply is, "There's probably some truth to what you say," and remain available to hear more information about that truth. Suppose that someone calls you "Stupid!" A possible reply is, "I have to agree that at times I've acted in a way that deserves the word 'stupid'; what in particular are you upset about?" Acknowledging possible truth is an alternative to becoming defensive, counterattacking, covering up or withdrawing.

Self-Disclosing

In chapters 6 and 7, the idea of communicating personal meanings in the "I" form was presented. Listener reactions to being criticized can be expressed in that way. For example, if you were criticized unjustly, you might reply: "When I hear you criticize me like that, I get angry at you." You might also include reference to your thoughts, intentions or other aspects of meaning, as appropriate. Self-disclosing serves as an alternative to becoming defensive, counterattacking, covering up or withdrawing.

Advantages of Self-Disclosing/Translating

Translating indicates acceptance of the speaker's words, and without acknowledging that facts conveyed are either right or wrong. Translating serves as a holding action, buying the listener time to determine what a good course of action might be. Translating allows the speaker to continue to speak and often results in a lessening of the attack. Translating indicates to the speaker that the communication has been accepted and understood. Thus, the speaker doesn't have to repeat or intensify the message in order to be heard.

Listener self-disclosure provides information as to what effect the speaker's communication has on that listener, and gives clear information about what the listener is thinking, feeling and wanting. Self-disclosing is a natural way for the listener to release feelings in a nondefensive and honest way. It facilitates the release of the listener's feelings in contrast to translating, which requires a temporary holding back of feeling in the interest of allowing the speaker to continue.

Both translating and self-disclosing avoid the problem of intensifying the conflict. Both take the criticism out of the realm of conflict and shift it into the realm of personal opinion, personal wants and mutual problem solving.

Adopting a Supportive Attitude

To deal more successfully with criticism and conflict, it may help to adopt a supportive attitude. By supportive, I mean forgiving people whose accusations are exaggerated or unjust because their words may be out of habit, not conscious choice. By supportive, I mean believing that people are better off working with each other than against each other. By supportive, I mean allowing yourself to care for other people in the sense that you would like their lives to work out even though you might disagree completely with what they say. By supportive, I mean withholding condemnation; I mean helping to uphold the dignity and self-esteem of all people, even adversaries.

It may be helpful for you to voice your understanding of the other's perception of the situation. For example, you could say, "From your position, I can see how you got upset," or "If I were in your shoes, I guess I might be mad too."

Dialogue

TLU: (Traditional Language User) When people are verbally attacked, they don't translate, adopt a supportive attitude and express their understanding of the attacker's position. They get mad and they fight back.

Author: I get it that you're taking issue with what I'm saying.

TLU: Yes, I am. The responses you're suggesting don't ring true. People aren't like that.

Author: I can understand why you would say that. What you read here doesn't fit your notion of what is practical. It doesn't fit with your experience of how people deal with criticism and conflict.

TLU: That's right.

Author: Looking at it from your viewpoint, I guess I'd have to agree with you. I wonder, though, if it has to be that way.

TLU: It doesn't have to, but learning new ways would be difficult, very difficult.

Constructive Ways of Dealing With Criticism and Conflict   131

Author: I hear what you're saying about being difficult and I wouldn't want to minimize that. I'm wondering, though, if it might not be worthwhile to consider alternative approaches. Conflict results in mental anguish, grief, loneliness and frustration. If people could find a better way to interact with each other, the rewards could be great, even though progress might be slow.

TLU: Another thing that I object to is the idea of admitting that your criticizers are right, when they really aren't. People have a right to defend themselves when they're attacked. You don't want people to be doormats for others to step on, do you?

Author: You're saying that people should stand up for themselves, instead of admitting to false charges, is that it?

TLU: Right on! I'm not going to let people put me down when what they are saying isn't true.

Author: I agree with you that people shouldn't be doormats. When people are attacked they do need to defend themselves. The question is whether or not words of criticism in fact constitute an attack that needs to be defended against. I guess that's where we differ. You see critical words as an attack, whereas I see them as a disguised expression of the speaker's personal meaning. You see critical words as indicating falsehoods about you. I see the same words as belonging only to the speaker. Speakers' words talk about them, not me. And, in my mind, speakers are entitled to their own opinions.

TLU: In our culture we've been brought up to take words seriously. We believe that we are entitled to fair treatment by others. We maintain self-respect in part by not allowing falsehoods about us to stand uncorrected. If someone calls you "lazy" and you're not, you have a right to be indignant, to deny the charge and to set the record straight.

Author: Yes, we've been brought up that way. And that's part of the problem. However, if we can find ways to avoid a lot of useless conflict over words, shouldn't we pursue them?

TLU: Oh yes, I think we ought to pursue them, but the road is rocky.

Author: You're right; it is a difficult undertaking. And there's still another problem that I'm sure you're aware of. That is, it is very difficult to translate, self-disclose and understand when you're already reacting emotionally to the other person. In that situation, I suggest that as soon as people become aware of how their emotional reaction are interfering, they replay the interaction in order to translate or self-disclose messages that earlier were communicated in a less effective way. As people become more aware of their emotional reactions and they practice translating and self-disclosing, they may be able to switch to translating and self-disclosing before a replay becomes necessary. It may not be readily apparent, but self-disclosure allows people to experience and express whatever emotions are current. Self-disclosure involves substituting one form of emotional expression for another and does not require repressing an emotion (which is not altogether healthy).

TLU: That's encouraging. What's next?

Changing Conflict to Cooperation

People in conflict have needs they would like to have satisfied. If Both were getting their needs met, they would tend to be less critical of each other. What is it that you could do, without suffering loss of self-respect, that would help your opponent's needs be met?

Sometimes the two of you have common goals (though in the heat of the moment, this may not be apparent). If you can identify common goals, it may be possible for both of you to move toward those goals, switching from conflict to cooperation.

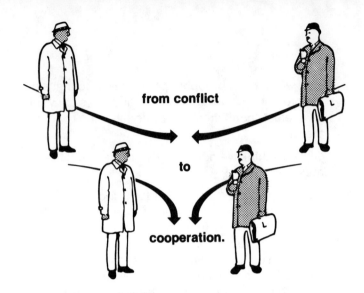

from conflict

to

cooperation.

In the following example, Father uses this principle.

Mother has criticized Father for being too lenient toward their son. Father has translated her message and come to understand her meanings more fully. He now knows that she wants him to check more carefully on the whereabouts of their son. Father is not willing to do that because he does not believe that it is appropriate. He voices his understanding of her position. "I can understand why you're critical of me, when I don't seem to be acting in our son's best interests." She nods in agreement. He goes on, "I'd like you to see that I care about him too. We have that in common. We both want our son to grow up to make good decisions and be a responsible adult." She nods. He continues, "I wonder how we can work together to make that happen?"

The same approach can be applied in a number of situations. Any two persons who are involved with each other usually have interests in common—the quality of the relationship, the success of a business, the winning of a game, the welfare of the family. Criticism from either person breeds conflict. Conflict obscures the fact that the two of them have common interests. Re-focusing on their common interests is a powerful way to move ahead in life.

Applying the Translating, Self-disclosing, Moving-Toward-Common-Goals Strategies

...and I thought I knew how to communicate!

In the first example that follows, Carol uses the strategies. In the second one, John does.

Husband/Wife

Joe: What's with this $60 check to Brown's Shoe Store?

Carol: You look annoyed.

Joe: I am! I see that you wrote a check for $60 to Brown's. You don't need shoes. You have a whole closet full of them.

Carol: You're angry with me for spending more money than you think I should have spent.

Joe: Look! We're trying to save money to buy a new house. We need every $60 we can get. We don't need to waste money.

Carol: (resists the temptation to defend her shoe purchase which she feels is fully justified, and replies) I can understand why you'd hate to see $60 go flying out the window. From your point of view, my buying shoes looks like a waste of money, like I'm not trying to help save money.

Joe: Every time I think we're starting to get ahead, things like this happen to set us back.

Carol: (to her, he seems less angry now) I can understand you feeling that way. I do too sometimes. I want that new house just as badly as you do. Though it may not look like it to you, I try not to waste any money at all. I look for sales. I compare prices when I shop. I don't buy luxuries. I really do want a new house. How can we make that dream come true? Let's look at the money situation and figure out how and what we can save in the next few months.

Joe: I'm embarrassed for reacting as strongly as I did. I realize now that I didn't even bother to ask if you really needed those shoes. Let's have a cup of coffee and talk some more about the house.

Employer/Employee

John is sitting at his desk drafting letters. In comes his supervisor waving a copy of a letter John had written to one of the firm's customers. In an angry tone of voice he demands, "Did you write this?" "Yes, Sir," John replies, somewhat concerned by his supervisor's manner.

Supervisor: Well, it's a lousy letter. If you can't do any better than that, I'll find someone who can. How could you write something so stupid?

John had been proud of this particular letter. He was upset by his supervisor's aggressive manner. He felt like he was being attacked. He reminded himself to listen, not defend.

John: I get it that you're pretty upset with me.

Supervisor: You're damned right I'm upset. Look at this (and he thrusts the letter in John's face).

John: What is it that particularly bothers you?

Supervisor: (pointing) These figures that you've quoted are incorrect, and the delivery dates are impossible. We're trying to get our operation back on its feet. Sending out this letter would bring down the wrath of the main office.

John now knows what his supervisor perceives to be the problem, and he knows that his supervisor wants to look good to the company's manager. John has a choice between continuing to translate feeling or identifying a common goal. He chooses the former because his supervisor still seems angry.

John: I can understand why you'd be upset. (John moves to stand beside his supervisor and they both look at the letter.)

Readers: (Note the significance of the physical move from against to beside.)

Supervisor: I. . . (hesitates, looking at John).

John: I mean, sir, that it makes sense that when you see a bad letter that you'd be upset.

...and I thought I knew how to communicate!

Supervisor: (somewhat perplexed as to what to say next, he repeats an earlier sentence in a more subdued voice) Sending out this letter would bring down the wrath of the main office.

John: (sensing that it's time for setting goals) You're interested in doing a good job and getting our division moving again. . . .

Supervisor: That's right, and just when I thought I had all the kinks ironed out, I see this.

John: (wants to identify goals they have in common and work cooperatively to reach them) Sir, I'd like this company to make a good profit too. My job means a lot to me. What do we need to do next?

Supervisor: As I said before, these figures and delivery dates are inaccurate and will cause us to lose money or miss deliveries.

John: May I assume that the rest of the letter is OK?

Supervisor: (nods) Except for the typos.

John: I think we can still impress the main office and get that new business we're after.

Now comes a delicate movement for John. He wants to avoid making his supervisor look silly. John had previously checked with the shipping department. They had said they could meet the delivery deadlines indicated in the letter. In regard to prices, he was following the suggestion made at a recent sales meeting that special incentive prices be quoted for select high-volume buyers.

John: I may be wrong, but I thought I remembered someone saying that price concessions for high quantity buyers would be acceptable on a trial basis. I thought that was a good idea at the time, and that it would help to keep this division moving toward profitability.

Supervisor: (sheepishly) Go on. (He realized that he had overreacted and that John is a competent employee acting in the best interests of the company.)

John: I know those dates look impossible, but before I change them, I'd like your permission to double check them with the shipping department to see if there is any possibility that they could be met. I'll clear up the typos with my secretary. She's quite competent. It may be that she thought all I wanted was a draft, not a final copy.

Supervisor: (nods)

John: I appreciate your pointing out errors when you see them. We all make mistakes at times. I'm pleased to know that I can count on you for feedback.

Supervisor: (apologetically) I guess I over-reacted. I think I've misjudged this letter and you. I've been on pins and needles lately because of some pressures at home. I guess I let some of that spill over on you.

John: I can understand that you must be under a great deal of pressure. I'm glad to have your help in getting this straightened out.

John felt very good about himself. He had been able to translate the criticism directed at him and to convey his understanding so well that his supervisor calmed down. He had identified goals toward which they could work cooperatively. He had maintained self-respect by handling this criticism skillfully, and he had avoided making his supervisor look bad (which his supervisor undoubtedly appreciates). John knew that he had actually improved his standing in the company with his skillful handling of a potentially destructive situation. He felt good about himself.

Practical Consideration

Possibly my examples seem too good to be true. In these dialogues, everybody gets something of what they want. People shift from attacking to cooperating; nobody gets hurt; no hard feelings result. Certainly not every potential conflict will turn out this way, but aren't results like that worth striving for?

Suppose that you don't succeed in your attempts to defuse a conflict. You get stuck in an emotional-reaction habit that sabotages your efforts. There is no reason to feel that all is lost.

When you become aware of what is happening, you can go back and re-shape the interaction, by employing some of the methods described here. If at this point you have difficulty directing the interaction towards mutual problem-solving, you can resort to more traditional ways of resolving differences—trading, yielding, demanding, avoiding, bargaining, taking and getting the services of a mediator or counselor. Most of us have had enough experience with these to know what they are, so that I won't go into detail here.

Criticizing and Starting Conflicts

Giving Feedback: An alternative to Criticizing

I haven't said much about starting conflicts because I don't believe in doing that. Neither do I believe there is much value in criticizing other people (though we all do that in the heat of anger). What I do believe in is self-disclosing and giving feedback. Recall that in Chapter 7, feedback was described as a process of sharing with the listener the speaker's reaction to something that listener had done. Feedback and criticism both communicate information, but there is a significant difference between them—*feedback emphasizes the speaker's reaction; criticism emphasizes the fault of the listener.*

That difference is clearly illustrated in the following example, in which Person B responds, in two different ways, to Person A (who has been repeatedly interrupting her).

Person B to Person A: (criticizing) You're rude and inconsiderate! You always interrupt me. You want all of the attention and you act like I'm not even good enough to tell a story. You make me look dumb in front of our friends!

Person B to Person A: (self-disclosing and giving feedback) I'd like you to be aware of something that's bothering me and getting in the way of our relationship. Several times in the past few weeks, I've started to tell a story but haven't been able to finish because you butted in and started to finish the story yourself.

When that happens I feel annoyed at you. I get embarrassed and I want to pull away from you. . . (waits for a reply)

As you may recall, there were practice exercises for giving feedback in Chapter 7. I suggest that you go back and review those. With practice, you'll learn to respond more quickly with feedback instead of criticism, when there is a problem between you and another person.

People have at least three choices when relationship problems emerge. One is to be silent, to swallow their feelings and try to accept the other person as is. Sometimes, people can do that successfully. Another choice is to criticize the other person, to point out the offending behavior in the strongest possible terms, in the hope that the other person will change. While this tactic may work, it often leads to resentment or retaliation by the other. The third option is to initiate a self-disclosure/feedback process, followed by a cooperative discussion of ways to resolve problems.

Regardless of which option you choose, try to allow any caring to emerge. Focus on how your relationship could be better, not merely on what is wrong with the other person.

In Closing

Clearly the techniques I have outlined won't solve all of the problems in the realm of human interaction. Real, sometimes unresolvable, conflicts exist between people. If someone with whom you are in conflict is determined to win at any cost, if that person insists on being right and doesn't want to cooperatively resolve differences, then I submit that there is little you can do to bring about change. It is, therefore, very important to translate (even if silently) the other's intentions. If you find out in the course of your interaction that the other person's intentions are hostile, then consider that further negotiation may be inappropriate. Consider that you may be dealing with an unchangeable situation, one which you must adjust to or leave in order to preserve your own interests. Consider these possibilities, but don't conclude that the situation is hopeless before giving the translation strategies a chance. They have been known to thaw ice.

Skill Builders

8.1 Translating: Responding to Criticism

Purpose:
To practice translating responses to criticism.

Directions:
Four different ways of translating criticism have been introduced—translating into thought and perception, translating into feeling, acknowledging some truth and translating into intention. Since the first three are considered to be good initial responses, why not take time to practice them? Below you'll find 7 criticisms directed at you. After each are three lines on which to respond with a translation into thought and/or perception (t), a translation into feeling (f), and an acknowledgement of some truth (at). I've filled in number one as an example.

1. Criticizer: "You don't care what happens to me"!
   (t)   "You're thinking that I don't care about you."
   (f)   "You sound angry at me."
   (at)   "I'll have to admit there are times when I haven't cared for you as much as I could have."

2. Criticizer: "You never listen."
   (t)   _____
   (f)   _____
   (at)   _____

3. Criticizer: "It's your fault."
   (t) _____
   (f) _____
   (at) _____

4. Criticizer: "Why don't you grow up!"
   (t) _____
   (f) _____
   (at) _____

5. Criticizer: "What made you think I'd be dumb enough to do that!"
   (t) _____
   (f) _____
   (at) _____

6. Criticizer: "You're always complaining!"
   (t) _____
   (f) _____
   (at) _____

7. Criticizer: "If it weren't for you, this wouldn't have happened!"
   (t) _____
   (f) _____
   (at) _____

...and I thought I knew how to communicate!

8.2 Self-Disclosing: Responding to Criticism

Purpose:
To practice self-disclosing responses to criticism.

Directions:
Recall a time when you were being criticized. Identify what went on with you in terms of your inner sensations, urges, feelings, perceptions, thoughts and wants. Make a brief statement that you could communicate to your criticizer. Include the phrase, "I get _____ when I see (hear) you _____ , and I think (want) _____." What you're working for are short, clear statements of your most important personal meanings. Too many words tends to dilute the impact.

Imagine how you think your criticizer might respond. Then translate that response.

Try this self-disclosing process in reference to other conflict situations you have experienced.

In Chapter 7, there were exercises in self-disclosing and giving feedback. It might be a good idea to look those over and practice them. With practice it becomes more natural for you to use these methods.

8.3 Converting Conflicts into Cooperation

Purpose:
To practice changing conflict to cooperation.

Directions:
Recall a recent conflict you had with someone who is important to you. Identify some of the wants you were experiencing when the conflict started. Identify some of the other person's wants; identify any goals that the two of you might have in common. What statements could you have made that would have identified your common goals and turned you both in the direction of cooperation?

_____

_____

_____

_____

_____

_____

_____

_____

_____

_____

_____

...and I thought I knew how to communicate!

8.4 Food for Thought

Purpose:
To sharpen understanding of the advantages and disadvantages of various ways of resolving conflicts.

Directions:
There are numerous strategies people use to deal with criticism and conflict. In addition to the translation/self-disclosing series proposed here, there are the more traditional methods of negotiating, taking, demanding, yielding, avoiding, tricking, trading and obtaining the services of a mediator or counselor. What advantages and disadvantages does each of these have? When might each be appropriate?

_____

_____

_____

_____

_____

_____

_____

_____

_____

_____

_____

_____

8.5 Conditions for Involvement in Conflict

Purpose:
To sensitize you to various conditions that work for or against the satisfactory resolution of conflict.

Directions:
When a situation involving criticism or conflict arises, try to create a positive environment for your interaction. Avoid trying to deal with the problem when conditions are unfavorable, for example, when you're likely to be interrupted or when you're tired.

For you and your "opponent," what are favorable times? places? personal conditions?

Imagine a possible conflict situation and plan how to include as many favorable aspects as possible.

...and I thought I knew how to communicate!

8.6 Verbally Responding to Criticism

Purpose:
To practice orally responding (in the recommended ways) to criticism.

Directions:
Write down in the space below 10-15 criticisms that you do not like to hear, that cause you to react defensively.

Recall the various strategies we've discussed so far—translating, obtaining more information, self-disclosing, verbalizing understanding of the other's point of view and turning in the direction of satisfying wants of both parties.

With those in mind, ask someone to direct toward you some of the criticisms from your list. Ask that person to sound and look as critical as possible, so you can practice using conflict reducing strategies.

1. _____

2. _____

3. _____

4. _____

5. _____

6. _____

7. _____

8. _____

9. _____

10. _____

...and I thought I knew how to communicate!

CHAPTER 9

Putting Your Self Into Your Life

In previous chapters, habitual ways of speaking and listening were contrasted with expressions of personal meaning. It was suggested that people need to become aware of their habitual ways and to develop skill in the use of personal-meaning alternatives. For listeners, an important skill is translating. Suppose a speaker remarks, "All Norwegians are flat headed." Instead of responding from habit, "You're crazy," a listener could translate and reply: "That's an interesting idea you have. Tell me more." When we have alternatives, we have more power to prevent conflict situations or to surmount them if they do develop.

Some of what you read here may seem strange to you, foreign to your natural inclinations for dealing with your world. Indeed, the meaning-making perspective does seem strange in comparison with our traditional patterns of response. We're faced with entrenched societal expectations about communication and with our own personal habits that resist change. To completely ignore these forces is out of the question; to completely follow them is self-defeating. Let's consider how to develop a middle ground. First, there is the possibility of communicating in traditional ways while thinking personal meanings. Second, there is the possibility of communicating traditionally when it seems to be effective to do so, then switching to personal meanings when it doesn't.

In some areas of your life, you no doubt communicate successfully. I assume you will continue in the same vein. In other areas of your life you may encounter problems. If it appears that your communication is not bringing about the results you intend, consider changing your perspective. Try something different (for example, a meaning-making alternative). I realize this is not easy. Time-honored habit is not easily displaced by a new substitute. If you've ever switched to a car with a clutch after driving one with an automatic transmission, you'll know what I mean.

In learning new ways, you'll likely run into opposition from habit. Your old habits of thinking will surely rally to the defense of the old ways. Your mind may make excuses ("I can't help it," "That's what everyone does," "It's natural to be that way.") Your mind may raise objections to the new, perhaps by calling it names like "awkward," "impractical" or "unnatural." Your mind may create fears ("What will people say," "Careful, I'll look silly,") as if trying something new would bring disaster. Be warned! Your habit thoughts will work against you.

When what you're currently doing isn't getting the results you need, try something different. *And you can try it even though habit raises fears and doubts.*

You May Need Some Help

Some of you may become aware of areas of your life that seem too big for you to handle by yourself. Well, that's what counselors, psychotherapists, psychologists and other "shrinks" are for. An investment in one of them might pay off. Find one that is competent and give the matter consideration. It's not true that you're "defective" if you go to see a counselor. What's true is that you were smart enough to realize that there was something you needed help with, and smart enough to seek professional assistance to deal with that.

Self

We have the potential to free ourselves from the grip of habit, to develop alternatives, and to exercise powers of choice because each of us has a **self-directing management system**—a center of awareness, a dynamic source of action and power—**a self**. I'm referring to the part of you that can consciously shift your gaze from this page to your body. . . . , that can become aware of your breathing . . . , that can raise your arm at will. . . , that can plan what to do next. . . , and that can do whatever is needed to integrate and direct the complex system that you are.

There is no doubt in my mind that we have this capacity for self-direction. Sometimes, however, we forget that; we start to feel less confident, less sure of ourselves.

Losing a Sense of Self

When we lose a sense of self, we are at the mercy of habit, other people and events. We may wonder who we are, become anxious or discouraged and unable to choose or act in our own best interests.

When I first saw Kathy she looked forlorn. Her body slumped in the chair. In a tired, discouraged voice she told me how she and her husband were fighting constantly and that on occasion he would hurt her. It was a great disappointment to her that her kids seemed to side with him much of the time. She had no relatives outside of her immediate family. Because of her attention to her children as they were growing up, she had not developed any close personal friends. She had been working part-time, which helped because it took her out of the home for a while each day, but she was let go when the firm lost much of its business. She had confided in their pastor and instead of getting emotional support, was told that divorce was out of the question. A woman's place was in the home. She said that she had lost her confidence and self-respect. From all that she said it become clear that she saw herself as a failure and as having no power to change things.

For people like Kathy, a positive sense of self may be lacking, but the potential for new action, for self-direction remains. She hadn't lost her ability to say "No," make new friends, seek a new job, find emotional support, love her children or make tough decisions about her husband. It just seemed that way because people and circumstances were making life difficult for her.

Regaining the Sense of Self-Power

One way to help people get in touch with their missing self-power is to have them recall a time when they felt successful in directing their lives.

I asked Kathy to recall a time when she felt good about herself, when things were going the way she wanted them to go, when she had energy, when she was making things happen for herself. I asked her to picture herself as she was then and to tell me what she looked like, what she was thinking and saying, how she was feeling. I asked her to become aware of the warmth, energy and aliveness she had experienced.

As she described in detail that time of feeling good, Kathy's body started to come back to life. Her face relaxed. She developed a smile. Her voice took on color and strength.

I asked her to more fully describe and to more deeply experience herself at that time.

I commented that she was beginning to look stronger now. She said that she was feeling much better, that she had somehow recovered some sense of feeling good about herself. She was struck by how different things seemed now than 30 minutes ago. Before, everything had seemed heavy; now it seemed light. Before, it had taken effort to make contact with me; now it came easily. She maintained good eye contact, seemed more alive and now felt ready to go out into the world and take care of her life. She had been powerful in the past and she had now regained a sense of that power. My job was to help her keep it.

Renewing a Sense of Self

If you have a strong sense that you have the potential to make your life work, great! You're in a good position to take from this book what can be helpful and to put it into practice as you see fit.

If you used to be confident about your potential but aren't now, the exercises at the end of this chapter should be helpful to you. When you regain your sense of self-direction you'll be in a stronger position to overcome the objections of habit and the demands of others so that you can change what you want to change.

If you've never had a clear sense of being able to direct your life, then it's time to develop it. The potential is within you; the rewards are great. The exercises at the end of this chapter can be practiced daily or until your positive sense of self starts to build and self-supporting habits replace your old habits of self-depreciation. Low self-esteem is a product of thinking, believing and feeling habits; it is a result of a certain way of thinking (not a truth). Recognize that you have a choice of thoughts. You can adopt those self-supporting thoughts that give you more satisfaction in place of those thoughts that habitually take that satisfaction away. You can adopt those thoughts that build your power to confront obstacles that stand in your way. You can replace out-worn communication habits with self-awareness, choice, intention and forward movement. What are you waiting for?

Skill Builders

Chapter 9: PUTTING YOUR SELF INTO YOUR LIFE

...and I thought I knew how to communicate!

9.1 Renewing Feelings of Self-Worth

Purpose:
To renew your sense of self-worth.

Directions:
Find a quiet spot where you can relax and where you can be free of distractions for a while. Let yourself relax. . . .

Recall a time when you really felt good about yourself. . . when you were doing what you wanted to do. . . when you had lots of energy. . . when things were going well for you. . . when you felt confident and strong. . . .

Let a moving picture come into your mind of what you were like then. . . . Notice what you were doing. . . and saying. . . . Look at your clothes, the colors, the people and the surroundings. . . . Become aware of what you were like in the picture. . . . Listen to what you and others are saying. . . . Hear the sound of your voice. . . . Notice what feelings you have. . . . Become aware of any warmth, tingling, energy, enthusiasm, aliveness you have. . .

Let that experience of feeling good about yourself come alive in your mind. . . Let yourself experience what you experienced then. . . . Let yourself feel the feeling good about yourself. . . . Let yourself become aware of warmth and energy and aliveness right now. . . . Stay with those feelings and experience them in your body. . . . Silently say to yourself:

"I have potential."
"I am capable of coping."
"I have the right to take care of myself."
"I have a source of power within me."
"I have within me ways of developing strength and energy."
"I am a continuing source of aliveness."

Write down those sentences in the space below.

Repeat those sentences aloud, firmly and with conviction!

Write down other phrases that re-affirm your own potential and power.

I am _____

I have _____

Make a drawing that symbolizes the energy, potential and power that you possess.

Repeat this activity within 24 hours.

Each of you is beautiful in your own way!

and don't forget!

...and I thought I knew how to communicate!

9.2 Recognizing Individual Accomplishment

Purpose:
To show how you can choose to make a positive assessment of self-accomplishment.

Directions:
In a competitive society like ours, people often learn to judge themselves on the basis of how they compare to others. Such judgments may be useful for some purposes. However, if these judgments are taken to be facts about one's degree of success in life, they can be detrimental to the development of a sense of self-power. Recognize that negative judgments are personal meanings and that alternate personal meanings are just as right (and probably more satisfying).

Sarah was asked what position she played in the band. In an apologetic voice she replied that although she had been playing for years, she was only third clarinet (a comparison with others that indicates a devaluing of herself.) What could Sarah have thought that was truthful and recognized the success of her efforts? Several things come to mind. (1) She played clarinet well, well enough to be selected for band. (2) In the process of practicing music, she learned habits of self-discipline that would help her in other ways. (3) She had learned a lot about music in general and band music in particular. (4) Her efforts contributed to the overall success of the band. (5) She had made good friends and she greatly enjoyed the feeling of being a functioning member of a group.

Sarah had clearly accomplished something for herself in her years of clarinet playing. She may only need to recognize this fact for her self-esteem to improve. This self-endorsing process could help her develop and maintain her sense of personal power.

In the following statements, the persons whose names are italicized are compared negatively to others. On the blank lines, write statements that point out personal gains or progress made by these persons who are being devalued.

1. **Frank** is the twelfth man on the twelve-man tennis team.

   _____

   _____

2. When your sister was your age she got all A's and now **you** come home with B's.

   _____

   _____

3. **She** can play the guitar, but nothing like Sis used to do.

   _____

   _____

4. My neighbor is lucky. He's got two cars but **I've** only got one. We could really use a second one but my wife doesn't have a good job like his does and we can't afford another. It isn't fair!

   _____

   _____

5. **He's** been playing football for three straight years and is still only second string tackle.

   _____

   _____

6. **He** missed 80 out of 100 on the test.

   _____

   _____

7. The **paper** boy has been late twice this month.

   _____

   _____

8. **I've** been living in this house for 10 years and we still have an old refrigerator.

   _____

   _____

Author's personal gain versions of the preceding statements.
1. This year Frank was good enough to get on the tennis team! or He's among the better players in the school.
2. When you get B's it's obvious you're learning the material! or, B's are certainly better than C's!
3. She can play the guitar!
4. You're doing OK. At least you have a car that runs!
5. He's made the football team three straight years now!
6. He got 20 right!
7. The paper boy has been on time 29 days this month!
8. You have a refrigerator that works!

9.3 Drawing Strength From What Others Have Done

Purpose:
To draw inspiration from stories of people who overcame great odds.

Directions:
People have potential to make their lives work.

Repeat that sentence and let the meaning soak in . . .

People have potential to make their lives work.

Can you allow yourself to believe that (even if you don't currently feel it or see it in others).

People have potential to make their lives work.

Another way of saying "have potential" is to say "have power." I have power, you have power, other people have power to help themselves move through life in constructive ways. The fact that we don't always use our power does not necessarily mean that we don't have it. A light that is turned off still retains the power to shine.

Having power does not mean being able to change everything one might want to change. Having power means having the capability to try again. It means making the best of what is and acting to make things better when that is possible.

Though there are times we may feel powerless, it is extremely rare that we actually lose all capacity to act in our own interests. Though circumstances may pull us down, we still retain the potential to cope and to rise again. The thousands of persons who survived starvation, deprivation, isolation, torture, filth, disease and back-breaking work in the Nazi concentration camps of World War II can attest to that. So can these others:

Ray Charles, who was born black and in poverty, who was later blinded, and who then became a star in the popular music field.

Ludwig van Beethoven, who wrote some of his greatest symphonies after becoming deaf.

...and I thought I knew how to communicate!

Glenn Cunningham, who after being burned so badly that the doctors feared he would never again walk, eventually set a world's record for the fastest mile.

Bill Wilson, who spent years as a hopeless alcoholic, and who later became the founder of Alcoholics Anonymous.

Franklin Delano Roosevelt, who faced the crippling effects of infantile paralysis, and who later became president of the United States.

Winston Churchill and **Albert Einstein,** who were discouraged from further schooling because they were labeled "stupid," and who later rose to world prominence as statesman and scientist.

Helen Keller, who overcame the stigma of deafness and blindness to help and inspire others who were handicapped.

There are others, many others, who never had the advantages of wealth, beauty, talent or influential friends, who never made the big time, yet who demonstrated a strength of character and a zest for life that is truly remarkable.

During my younger days, Herb and I played in a combo in a night club in southern Wisconsin. Herb carried quite a burden. In the first place, he was black. That meant being socially isolated, living on the wrong side of the tracks and working at whatever leftover jobs whites didn't want. His wife was sick, leaving Herb to rear their children. To make ends meet, he had to work three jobs. By day he was a janitor, in the evening a maintenance man, and from 10 p.m. to 2 a.m. Friday and Saturday nights, a musician. When he wasn't working, Herb kept house, raised his family and visited his sick wife. The drain on his pocketbook, time and energy was tremendous.

Perhaps the cruelest slap of all was that Herb's musical talent went unrecognized. The dingy nightclub in which we played on weekends was the only place within sixty miles that regularly hired a band. The choice was play there or not play at all. And in that noisy place, where people seemed more interested in drinking and fighting than listening and dancing, his talent was wasted.

All of this was enough to drive many people to the brink of despair, but not Herb. In the years that I knew and worked with him, I heard few complaints or expressions of bitterness. His inner strength and positive attitude held that combo together and still provide some of my warmest memories. I continue to draw strength from him.

We have all known individuals who possess a sense of personal power and who demonstrate that in their interactions with others. Recall such a person. . . . That person may be someone you read about, may have been portrayed in a movie or on television, or may have played an actual part in your life. Let the qualities of that person come vividly into your mind. . . . Get in touch with the energy that person possesses, the determination, the willingness to continue, to try again and move ahead. . . . Whatever qualities you think of, repeat those qualities to yourself as you recall that powerful person. . . . Let yourself imagine how you could become more like that person. . . . Imagine yourself assuming some of the positive qualities of that person, some of the energy, some of the enthusiasm, some of the determination. . . . Become aware of how you stop yourself from attaining more of those qualities. . . . Imagine how you could move ahead to become more like a person with power. . . . Remind yourself that this was possible for that person and that it is possible for you. Actually you already possess power, and need only to realize and develop it.

From time to time recall a person with power and repeat the process described in this activity.

9.4 Increasing Positive Self-evaluation Through Doing

Purpose:
To provide a method for increasing positive thoughts about self.

Directions:
Below is a list of actions that are typically perceived as worthwhile. Put a check in front of each one that you perceive as worthwhile and which you could do in the next few days.

_____ share something of yourself with somebody.
_____ make friends with someone new.
_____ present your point of view to others.
_____ say something positive to someone else.
_____ take time to do something for yourself.
_____ learn something new.
_____ try something new.
_____ do something to improve the environment.
_____ not gossiping when you could.
_____ increase a skill by practicing.
_____ do something positive for someone else.
_____ relax yourself.
_____ activate yourself.
_____ do something that you have put off.
_____ be kind or thoughtful to someone.
_____ help someone else deal with a problem.
_____ be self-observing.
_____ be accepting or tolerant.
_____ shrug off a put-down,
_____ try to understand someone else's view.
_____ help someone else learn.
_____ do something to help a relationship.
_____ smile.
_____ tell yourself you did something right.
_____ meet an obligation.
_____ plan ahead.

It stands to reason that if you perform worthwhile actions, you could think positive thoughts about yourself for having performed these actions. Thinking positive thoughts about yourself is one way to increase you sense of self-worth. Why not get started right now? After each action is complete, give yourself recognition for completing a worthwhile act.

Postscript

You have had the opportunity to 1) become aware of some habits that lead to conflict and misunderstanding, 2) learn some alternative ways of speaking and listening, 3) develop alternate viewpoints on communication, 4) practice various techniques, and 5) strengthen your ability to make choices about relating with others. I assume that if you read, thought about and practiced, you are now capable of making some changes in the ways you interact with others. i assume, too, that there are still other changes that you (and the rest of us) could make.

With the possible other changes in mind, I'm listing various books that develop the ideas, techniques and viewpoints presented here. I have found each of these books to be useful for myself and in working with others. Best wishes to you as you journey through life.

...and I thought I knew how to communicate!

List of References

Alberti, R.E. & Emmons, M.L. *Your perfect right* (3rd ed.). San Luis Obispo, CA: Impact, 1978.

Assagioli, Roberto. *Psychosynthesis.* New York: Viking Press, 1965.

Bandler, R. & Grinder, J. *Frogs into princes.* Moab, UT: Real People Press, 1979.

Bolton, Robert. *People skills.* Englewood Cliffs, NJ: Prentice-Hall, 1979.

Brown, Molly. *The unfolding self.* Los Angeles, CA: Psychosynthesis Press (distributed by Intermountain Associates for Psychosynthesis, 60 Isleta Drive, Los Alamos, NM 85744), 1983.

Condon, J.C. *Semantics and communication* (2nd ed.). New York: Macmillan, 1975.

Dobson, Terry & Miller, Victor. *Giving in to get your own way.* New York: Delacorte Press, 1978.

Ellis, Albert & Harper, Robert. *A new guide to rational living.* Hollywood, CA: Wilshire Books, 1975.

Fabun, Don (ed.). *Communications.* (Reprinted and distributed by International Society for General Semantics, PO Box 2469, San Francisco, CA 94126), 1965.

Gordon, Thomas. *Parent effectiveness training.* New York: Peter H. Wyden, 1970.

Johnson, D.W. *Reaching out* (2nd ed.). Englewood Cliffs, NJ: Prentice-Hall, 1981.

Johnson, Wendell. *People in quandaries.* (Reprinted and distributed by International Society for General Semantics, PO Box 2469, San Francisco, CA 94126), 1946.

Maltz, Maxwell. *Psycho-cybernetics.* New York: Pocket Books, 1969.

Miller, Sherod, Nunnally, E.W. & Wackman, D.B. *Couple communication 1: Talking together.* Minneapolis, MN: Interpersonal Communication Programs, 1979.

Stevens, John. *Awareness: Exploring, experimenting, experiencing.* New York: Bantam Books, 1973.

Table of Skill Building Activities

Skill building activities provide opportunities to develop knowledge, awareness and interpersonal skills through experience. Various kinds of activities are included: observations, self-awareness, imagery, role playing, analysis of situations, discussion, problem solving and practice techniques. In each chapter some activities can be done alone; others are for two or more persons.

...and I thought I knew how to communicate!

Chapter 9: PUTTING YOUR SELF INTO YOUR LIFE

...and I thought I knew how to communicate!